Praise for *Raising*

"How do we create a future in which all of our children can truly flourish? The white among us choose to do differently with our kids than was done with us - with commitment, clarity and love. *Raising Antiracist Kids* is an accessible, direct, and necessary resource for parents of white children longing for a world of justice and mutuality. Read it. Engage it. Share it with a friend."
- **Jennifer Harvey**, PhD., author of *Raising White Kids: Bringing Up Children in a Racially Unjust America*

"Rebekah Gienapp beautifully bridges the latest research on how children observe and absorb race/ism with the informed practice of antiracist parenting. As a parent of color and antiracism curriculum specialist who regularly works with 'beginners' to active antiracism, I am thrilled to present *Raising Antiracist Kids* to my communities of parents and teachers, knowing that they will find Rebekah's content approachable and empowering."
- **Lucretia Carter Berry**, PhD., Founder of Brownicity.com: Many Hues, One Humanity

"*Raising Antiracist Kids* synthesizes current research to explain in down-to-earth language why white children are likely to develop racially prejudiced beliefs. Author Rebekah Gienapp helps parents counter this trend with thoughtful suggestions for parent-child conversations, well-organized by child age and topic. Her recommendations for family action steps are practical and her personal journey is moving. Readers will be inspired to openly examine and challenge white privilege in their families and communities."
- **Marietta Collins**, PhD. and **Ann Hazzard**, PhD., authors of *Something Happened in Our Town: A Child's Story about Racial Injustice*

"There's so much to love about Rebekah Gienapp's short book. Its tons of practical advice that engage some of the most commonplace and difficult challenges caregivers face. The many stories from her personal experience as a child and mother. The accessibility of the ideas and language. The organization of the book by developmental stages. Most strikingly, Rebekah is as generous in sharing the many "mistakes" along her path to raising an antiracist son as she is with her wise advice, and in doing so she imparts arguably the most crucial lesson of all. To paraphrase Maya Angelou: do your best, and when you know better, do better. If you're a white parent to white children and pay attention to this excellent book, you'll do better."
- **Andrew Grant-Thomas**, PhD., co-founder, EmbraceRace

"Rebekah offers us a great gift in these pages as parents and practicing antiracists. She offers a resource rich, age specific guide for parents to integrate antiracist approaches into our parenting and lives. But more than that, she creates a vulnerable and welcoming space in her writing and ideas, inviting us as white parents to make mistakes, show up anyway and learn alongside our children. The result is as much a learning guide for parents as it is for white adults committed to creating a different kind of world where whiteness is examined and white supremacy is addressed and dismantled with an inside/outside approach to action and practice."
- **Jardana Peacock,** author of *Practice Showing Up: A Guidebook for White People Working for Racial Justice*

Raising Antiracist Kids

An age-by-age guide for parents of white children

Rebekah Gienapp

In memory of Brandon Webber.
Rest in power.

CONTENTS

Part I
Why antiracist parenting is needed

My first memories of race

I grew up in Memphis, Tennessee in the 1980's. It's a majority Black city with a long legacy of white racism and racial segregation that felt intense in my childhood years.

The public elementary school I attended was probably about 80 percent Black students and 20 percent white students. My school was the only place I spent time where I wasn't in the racial majority as a white person. The first time I remember someone referring to my race was in second grade.

It was a cold morning, so students were allowed to come into the building's entryway while we waited for the bell to ring. It was hot and crowded. Suddenly, I got a terrible feeling. I threw up— and not just a little bit. A lot. Vomit landed on my binder, and even in my best friend's hair. It was mortifying, especially because everyone saw it.

A few days later, I was walking down the hall to the bathroom. I heard a Black girl I didn't know telling another kid in a loud whisper, "that's that honky who threw up in the hallway."

I felt so embarrassed. Now, I didn't like being

called a honky. I knew it wasn't a positive word. But I think I was more upset that she remembered I threw up! I knew honky was a racial insult, but the sting of it faded fairly quickly. The sting of being the girl who vomited in the hallway lasted a long time.

A year or so later, I had a very different racial experience.

I went to spend a week with my grandparents who lived in a small town in rural western Tennessee. My great aunt, who I rarely spent time with alone, took me on an outing for the day. On our drive back to my grandparents' house, she chose a route I didn't remember taking before.

Pointing to a group of Black children playing outside, she turned to me and said, "Do you know what we call that place?" I shook my head. She made sure to catch my eye before she told me: "that's n----r hill."

I remember being flooded with shame and freezing up in silence. I can still re-play the moment in my mind, watching two children running across a yard just before hearing that awful word come out of her mouth.

The sting of that moment didn't fade. It made me want to avoid my great aunt. I felt ashamed that we were related. The truth is, I never shook those feelings, even as an adult.

As a child I couldn't have articulated the difference between these two racial insults, my aunt using the n-word and me being called a honky. But the feelings in my body and heart told me they were two very different things.

Confusing childhood messages

I had plenty of other racialized childhood experiences. But I was also growing up in a time when many white liberals hoped that racism was becoming a thing of the past.

Even though my parents didn't tell me I should be colorblind, lots of other sources did. My high school even had a club called Colorblind, designed to promote racial harmony. Perhaps the fact that only 1 of the 40 students who joined the club was white should have raised questions about whether it was possible to be colorblind.

Growing up, I received many contradictory messages about race from the conversations I overheard and the behavior that I witnessed.

There were my great aunt's racist digs that became a staple of our family's Thanksgiving dinners, along with the turkey and dressing. I think she hoped to get a reaction from my mother, who taught at an all-Black elementary school.

At church, we learned that God made all of us. But when church leaders planned an ice cream social with a Black sister church in our denomination, some of the older members at our all white church were angry about it.

At home, we often compared our family favorably to suburban white people. We criticized them for avoiding majority Black schools and laughed at how they were afraid to spend time in most neighborhoods of our city. But my parents also talked a lot about crime, and we were taught to always keep ourselves locked inside of cars and houses.

I heard a lot about white people and thought of myself as white, but I had no idea what my ethnic heritage might be. I never even realized that some white people knew their ethnicity until I attended college in Iowa. Almost everyone seemed to know they were Dutch, German, or Norwegian.

The childhood messages I received about race from home, school, church, and the media were often confusing and contradictory.

However, these confusing messages did come together to tell me something important: race mattered.

It mattered a lot, and there was no pretending otherwise. Even if the media—and a lot of adults in my life—told me to be colorblind, at some level I already knew that wasn't possible.

What research tells us

Some of my childhood experiences, like attending majority Black schools, aren't common for white people. But I wasn't a unique child in noticing that race was a big deal. Research tells us that children do notice race, and try to make sense of it, from very young ages.

I write often about race and kids, and more than a few of my white readers have told me that children are innocent. Some have suggested that kids don't perceive race or prejudice until adults point it out to them.

Sometimes we don't realize that our children are making race related observations because their questions or comments are subtle. We have to keep in mind that not all race talk is explicitly about prejudice.

Another factor affects what children say to parents

about race, and what they don't. If an adult in a child's life has become uncomfortable when they made a race related comment, and responded with "that isn't important" or "that's not polite to talk about," the child learns to keep their race talk out of adult earshot.

White people are also socialized to think of ourselves as not having race. We're often unaware of the many ways our experiences, and our children's experiences, are being shaped by whiteness. Being able to keep our children in majority white spaces most of the time is a racial experience. That experience builds our white children's expectations of what the world is like, whether we realize it or not.

Many white parents believe that if we don't talk to our kids about race, they won't see race and they won't develop prejudices.

But that's just not true. Consider this:

- One study found that toddlers as young as two years old used racial categories to explain people's behavior.

- A number of studies have found babies are able to categorize people by race by the age of three to six months.

Several studies have found that children's racial beliefs are not consistently related to their parents' beliefs, indicating that kids' ideas about race are influenced by many different sources.[1]

As the website of the American Psychological Association's RESilience Initiative states, "Children are learning about race and ethnicity whether they talk about them or not. Even choosing not to directly discuss race communicates your values and beliefs."[2]

What's the bottom line that caregivers need to understand? Our children notice race from early ages. They're trying to make sense of what they notice. **But without explicitly antiracist guidance from adults, they will often misinterpret the differences they notice.**

If we don't talk to kids early and often about race, those misinterpretations can develop into racism.

What the colorblind approach gets wrong

There are many reasons to reject colorblind ideology. Racism is a huge problem in our society. How are we supposed to tackle that problem if we don't talk about race? We don't tell kids to challenge gender bias by never talking about or noticing someone's gender.

When we stay silent about race around our kids, or when we tell them that race doesn't matter, we leave them to draw their own conclusions.

Imagine, for example, a white, middle-class child who is told repeatedly that "everyone is equal" and "everyone is the same on the inside." Her parents don't give her any other information about race.

They also emphasize that they work hard for the things their family has. She should appreciate those things, her parents tell her, and treat them carefully because of the hard work it took to get them.

Even though her parents aren't talking about race, this child will notice ways that everyone isn't equal.

On a drive her parents make through a working class Latinx neighborhood, she might observe how much smaller the houses are compared to the ones in her white middle-class neighborhood.

Her parents often talk about how glad they are that she's able to go to a "good school" in a "safe neighborhood." As she looks around her classroom, she notices that there is only one Black child in her class.

Since her parents encourage her to be colorblind by what they do and say, she's learned not to ask them questions about what's behind the differences she's noticing.

Perhaps she'll think that the parents in the Latinx neighborhood don't work hard like her parents, and that's the reason why their houses are smaller. After all, if everyone is equal and people get nice things through hard work, that explanation makes sense a child.

She may decide that most Black kids aren't smart enough to go to a school as "good" as hers. Maybe she's even overheard a few adults imply that's the case.

A young child in this situation is forming what Louise Derman-Sparks and Julie Olsen Edwards refers to as *pre-prejudice*. If caregivers address her misinformation soon enough, it can be corrected before it becomes a prejudice.[3] But if her caregivers never talk about race, there's no opportunity to correct those false beliefs.

A colorblind approach to raising and educating kids is harmful for both children of color and white children. It contributes to white children believing that they and their white peers must deserve the unjust privileges they have. Instead, we need to teach them that these privileges result from living in a racist, unjust society.

When parents start talking about race

One study of white families asked parents to talk

openly about race and interracial friendships with their young children. The researcher found that when parents did this, the children greatly improved their racial attitudes and reduced their prejudice.

The catch? Even though there were 100 white families in the study, only six of the families were willing and able to talk explicitly about interracial friendship. The others either skirted around the topic, failed to have any conversation at all, or dropped out of the study.

Many of the parents admitted to the researcher that they either didn't know what to say to their children, or they were afraid to say the wrong thing.[4]

Dropping the colorblind approach is challenging for many white caregivers. But if we want children to be able to challenge racism, they've got to be able to talk about race.

One study about children's literature is revealing. Researchers divided children into two groups, each of which read a different version of a storybook. One version was colorblind, while the other explicitly talked about valuing diversity.

Researchers found that the children who read the book that explicitly talked about race were much more able to identify racial discrimination, even when it was presented in subtle forms.[5]

Is multiculturalism enough to combat racism?

Many schools and families have chosen a multicultural approach over colorblind ideology as they talk about race with kids. Multiculturalism offers some distinct advantages to the colorblind approach. It celebrates the identities and cultures of Black, American Indian, Latinx, and Asian American children. This gives children of color opportunities to feel seen and affirmed.

Multicultural books are often described as "mirrors" for children of color, helping combat negative portrayals and invisibility that they encounter elsewhere. Multiculturalism also expands the awareness that all kids have about cultures that aren't their own. Multicultural books serve as "windows" that help kids look into and understand other people's lives.

But as antiracism writer Dr. Jennifer Harvey points out, multiculturalism alone isn't enough. She reminds us that the society we're raising our kids in isn't simply racially diverse.

Our kids live in a diverse society that also operates as a white racial hierarchy. White people have power and privilege that people of color do not. Multiculturalism doesn't address these racial power dynamics, so this strategy is not enough (by itself) to undo racism.[6]

There are other ways that multiculturalism can be problematic. Depending on how it's implemented, multicultural celebrations can reinforce ideas kids have that whiteness is "normal," while Black, Latinx, Asian, and Native American peoples are "fascinating" or "exotic."

Embracing antiracist parenting

The colorblind approach to parenting is harmful. The multicultural approach to parenting isn't a full solution. But antiracist parenting can equip our kids to identify and challenge racism.

In his ground-breaking book *How To Be An*

9

Antiracist, Dr. Ibram X. Kendi highlights how in the age of Trump, many people proclaim that they are "not racist." Kendi asks:

> *What's the problem with being "not racist?" It is a claim that signifies neutrality: "I am not a racist, but neither am I aggressively against racism." But there is no neutrality in the racism struggle. The opposite of "racist" isn't "not racist." It is "antiracist."*[7]

Kendi describes antiracism as standing firmly on the side of racial equality rather than blaming racial groups for the injustices they face.

Antiracism proclaims that racism is primarily dismantled by challenging racist power and policies. An antiracist person, Kendi tells us, is someone "supporting an antiracist policy through their actions or expressing an antiracist idea."[8]

Perhaps you're wondering about how Kendi's understanding of antiracism could apply to children. If antiracism is about challenging policies and power, how can children do that? Are we talking about coercing our children into taking action against racism?

I don't believe that forcing children to do things is healthy in any aspect of parenting. Whether we're talking about social justice or developing healthy eating habits, coercion often backfires.

Here's what I do know—our children are surrounded by racist ideas and policies that influence their thinking. From the way education systems are organized, to the stereotypes that flood children's media, to the unintentionally racist things we've done in their presence, our kids are being shaped by racism.

If we don't want our kids to embrace racist ideas,

10

we must surround them with antiracist ideas. We must provide them with the coaching and support that equip them to take antiracist action when they are ready.

That looks different for my 21-year-old stepson than it does for my 7-year-old son. What I say and do today with my 7-year-old is different from how we talked about race and racism at age four.

But white parents should not wait until our children reach a particular age to start talking, thinking, and acting in antiracist ways.

Why this book focuses on white children

When it comes to racism, white people spend most of our time in a state of denial:

- Denial about how each of us, whether we want to or not, benefit from racism.
- Denial about how the choices we make, including parenting choices, often uphold systemic racism.
- Denial about the ways that racism still influences our thinking and our actions.

We're also much less likely to talk to our children about race and racism than parents of color.

Most of us didn't witness many antiracist conversations as children. If we want to break the patterns of white silence and denial in the face of racism, we must start with our children.

I've also chosen to focus on parenting white children in order to "stay in my own lane." I'm not the parent of a child of color. I can't teach about experiences I do not have.

I realize that there may be white adults reading this book who parent both white children and children of color. I encourage you to seek out some of the many helpful bloggers and writers who talk about how they navigate race in their multiracial families, such as Diedre Anthony, Lucretia Berry, Rachel Garlinghouse, and Rorri Geller-Mohamed.

What antiracist kids can do

Children who understand that race matters are kids who are better equipped to challenge racism. When caring adults talk to white kids honestly about the difference race makes in our lives and in society, so much can happen.

Talking about race and racism guards against white children developing a false sense of racial superiority. Without these conversations, white kids are likely to assume that they deserve the privileges and advantages whiteness gives them, instead of understanding these privileges as unjust.

Children who are comfortable talking about race and have practiced noticing racial discrimination will be able to speak up about everything from racial teasing to inaccurate history lessons.

Antiracist parenting doesn't just shape our children; it also shapes us. **Conversations with my children have challenged me to wrestle with the racism that still lives inside my own mind, heart, and body.**

My desire to help my kids become antiracist strengthens my own commitment to antiracism. I can't ask my children to do what I'm not doing myself.

12

How to use this book

This book is primarily organized by age group to help parents focus on the specific conversations and experiences that children are more likely to have at each developmental stage. However, I highly recommend that you at least skim all the parts, even if your kids are older or younger than the group addressed in that section.

Why? **Because children's understanding of race and racism can vary widely at each age, depending on what their experiences have been.**

A 12-year-old who knows few people of color and has been discouraged from talking about race in the past could benefit from modified versions of some of the strategies I share in part III for preschool age children.

An 8-year-old who lives in a racially diverse neighborhood and whose parents take them to protests might already be struggling with guilt about being white. That's a topic that I cover in part V for middle school children.

Also, many of the ideas I'm sharing can be used with more than one age group (with some modification, of course). To avoid being repetitive, I've chosen a specific age group to feature each strategy.

You'll also notice that in each section there are practices that you can try with your child. A practice is just what it sounds like: a chance to try something new, and then practice it again. Some are opportunities to try new ways of talking with our kids about race. Other are strategies we can use to help kids take antiracist action.

The final chapter of the book focuses on our own antiracism work. We have important work to do as adults, and we need to model antiracist commitment to our children.

I also talk about emotional and spiritual resources that help us stay in this work for the long haul. Frustration and burnout are common as we challenge racism, but there are ways we can resist these tendencies.

Raising white children to be antiracist is not easy. It's common to struggle with many different emotions while doing this work. If you begin to feel overwhelmed as you work through this book, I encourage you to take breaks and do something that feeds your soul. Perhaps you will journal, pray, meditate, play, do yoga, or spend time in nature.

If you feel like you're "behind" or "you've already messed up," remember this: **our children don't need us to be perfectly antiracist ourselves before we can start this work with them.**

We can learn alongside them. We may even find that their courage will inspire our own.

Pause and Reflect

Consider how your own childhood experiences shaped your understanding of race, using the worksheet in my free *Raising Antiracist Kids* bonus pack. Download the pack at antiracistkids.com

Part II
Antiracist parenting in the toddler years

If you Google "how to talk to kids about race," you'll notice that most of the articles start with the preschool years (or later). But there are many things that parents and caregivers can do in the toddler years to help little ones make sense of what they are noticing about race.

In the introduction, I briefly mentioned that research shows babies as young as six months old notice racial differences. How did researchers measure this? They showed Black and white babies photographs of faces, measuring how long their attention stayed on each photo.

Looking at a photograph longer meant that a baby's brain found the face out of the ordinary and was trying to make sense of what the baby saw. The study found that babies looked significantly longer at photographs of a person whose race was different than their parents' race.[9]

Of course, this doesn't mean that babies are prejudiced. It does mean that they are noticing a difference. As they grow, they'll try to make sense of the differences they note.

Babies will also imitate the race related behavior and language of the adults in their lives as they grow older. After all, toddlers are excellent imitators!

Therefore, what we say, what we do, and who we include in their lives will influence how they interpret race.

Noticing skin color and labelling race

One of toddlers' important developmental tasks is learning the language they need to label their worlds. That's why parents may be asked 100 times a day "what's that?"

Caregivers can help children with this labelling by noticing differences in skin tone, hair texture, and eye shape. This should include naming white children's skin tones, hair textures, and other physical characteristics, as well as those of Black, Latinx, Asian, and indigenous peoples. Otherwise, we send children the unspoken message that "normal" skin is white, and therefore doesn't need to be named.

As white parents and caregivers, we also need to guard against exoticizing children of color's skin tones or other physical characteristics.

Several years ago, I was visiting with a preschool director in preparation for a book fair we would be doing together. When I showed her the book, *We All Went on Safari*, a story set in Tanzania, she told me how much she liked the book because of how dark the children's skin was.

Something about the way she said it left me unsettled, wondering what she might be saying to the Black students in her childcare center about their skin.

We also need to go beyond describing skin tones to introducing the racial labels society uses.

Correlating race and skin tone is confusing for children at first, but it can be done.

In part III, we'll talk more about how to help kids correlate skin tone and racial labels like Black and white.

But for now, just introducing these words into your toddler's vocabulary is helpful. They'll be better able to ask you questions about their perceptions of skin color and race if they have this vocabulary.

Kim Sherman, who is a white parent, gave one example of this on the blog *Raising Race Conscious Children*. When she was pregnant, Sherman knew that her 2-year-old would ask her lots of questions about the baby who was coming. But she was surprised when her toddler asked, "Will be the baby be Black or White?" Later, Sherman realized that her toddler probably asked because she had two baby dolls, one Black and one white.

Young children don't know where skin color comes from. So, Sherman told her "The baby's skin will probably look like yours and mine and Daddy's skin, the peachy color we call White." She also reminded her daughter that some families include people with many different skin colors.[10]

Naming skin tone and race at home regularly, like Sherman's family does, also gives toddlers a chance to voice any misconceptions they have. This gives us the opportunity to gently correct them, hopefully before they make remarks that could hurt the feelings of a child of color. Even children whose caregivers are committed to antiracism will still sometimes make mistakes at school and in the community. But we can reduce how often this happens through the conversations we have at home.

Practice: Naming skin tone and race with your toddler

There are many times and settings that allow parents to easily name skin tone and race with our toddlers, including:

- While we're cuddling our children. For example, "I notice that your skin is peachy. Mine is a little darker. I think of it as light tan. We both have skin that people call white."

- While reading a book, such as *Brown Bear, Brown Bear, What Do You See?* Even though the final page of the book shows children of many different races, this isn't commented on. We can encourage our kids to name the colors they see, just like they did on the other pages of the book. (I learned this idea from the fantastic kid activist group Wee the People Boston.)

- For kids who have dolls of more than one race, we can ask them how they would describe the different skin tones. We can help them learn some of the racial labels our culture uses as well, with statements like, "Yes, his skin is copper brown. If he were a real person, he looks like he might be Latino. That means his ancestors are from Mexico, South America or Central America."

Surrounding toddlers with diverse learning resources

As a children's bookseller, parents often ask me for books that can help a child work through a particular challenge. One day I ran into a white customer who was concerned about a pattern she'd noticed with her toddler. When her daughter was around Black people at places like the playground, she seemed afraid of them.

My customer had recently bought new baby dolls for her toddler, including a lighter brown skinned doll and a darker brown skinned doll. Her toddler didn't want to play with either of them. But her mother was wisely continuing to "nurture" and play with the dolls herself, suspecting that eventually this would rub off on her daughter.

We also talked about book recommendations. She already knew that reading books about different kinds of animals getting along wouldn't be enough to challenge her daughter's pre-prejudice.

She said she needed toddler books with Black, Latinx, Asian, and white characters so that her child could make the explicit connections to the people she saw in her world.

We talked about some book ideas. When we ran into each again a few months later, she said her daughter's fear had receded.

It took a sustained effort on her part, reading and discussing diverse books and playing with the dolls. It took more than one book and more than one toy, but eventually her toddler's pre-prejudice subsided.

Tips for avoiding stereotypes
in books and toys

Not all racially diverse books and toys are equally valuable. Here are some tips for choosing toys and books that will fight stereotypes instead of reinforcing them. Parents can:

- Make sure our homes have <u>many</u> toys and books that represent people of color. If 95% of the stories in their home library have white main characters, children will still get the idea that white is "normal," standard, or best.

- Look for books that show kids and adults of color engaged in everyday activities. Toddlers are very interested in practical, daily aspects of life. We want children to respect and appreciate other cultures, not focus on them as exotic.

- Look for books where Asian, Latinx, Black, and indigenous people are the main characters, not just the sidekicks. Two examples are *Please, Baby, Please* by Spike Lee and Tonya Lewis Lee or *Toddler Two* by Anastasia Suen.

- Buy dolls that were made by people of color and read books that were written by people of color whenever possible. See the resource section at the end of the book for ideas.

- Avoid toys and books that communicate stereotypes about people of color. Many "global" games and toys do this by primarily picturing how people dressed in the past, such as Chinese people wearing rice paddy hats. It's also very common for Native American peoples to be portrayed only in the past.

For toddlers and preschoolers, it's especially important to focus on present day life.

- Label countries and cultures. When a story takes place in another country, or your toddler finds an object in your home from another culture, tell them where it's from. You might feel a bit silly at first saying "this song is from Thailand" to a 2-year-old. But it helps give them the background knowledge that gradually builds cross-cultural understanding.

- Look for books that include many different kinds of families, no matter who makes up your family. Kids can often get the idea that children are supposed to "match" their parents in terms of skin tone. As we read, we can point out how some families share the same skin color, and others don't. Parents can remind kids that it's love that makes a family. One book that can start these conversations are *Barefoot Books Baby's First Words* by Christiane Engel.

- Avoid play tipis. While play tents are fun, play tipis communicate stereotypical images about Native Americans rooted in the past. They contribute to lumping the very diverse 500+ federally recognized Native American nations into one culture. Ask a non-Native preschooler where they think Indians live today, and it's likely they'll say in a tipi. We need to counter the harmful narratives about American Indians found in children's literature and in our broader culture.

What if you feel like you've already made a mistake?

Another mom asked me recently what we should do when we realize that we've already introduced a stereotype with our children. That's a great question, because the truth is that it's not a matter of what to do **if** we make a racist mistake. The question is what we to do **when** we realize we made a racist mistake.

None of us are perfect, and we are all shaped by racism. It often takes time and self-reflection to realize how we've perpetuated a stereotype.

When my son was a toddler, I loved reading Dr. Seuss to him. *The Cat in the Hat* was one of our favorite books. For his first birthday my mother and I even made him an elaborate topsy-turvy cake that looked like the Cat's hat.

By the time our kiddo was four, I'd done enough reading about Dr. Seuss to know that some of his work was openly racist. Once I knew that the Cat character was based on a blackface actor, I was deeply unsettled.[11]

My first step was dealing with my own shame,

which was rooted in the false idea that it's possible to avoid ever making a mistake. I am encouraged by what Oprah Winfrey says Maya Angelou once told her about mistakes she made as a younger adult. Angelou said to her, "You did in your twenties what you knew how to do, and when you knew better you did better."[12]

Next, I decided to tell my son what I had learned. I told him that when Dr. Seuss created the Cat character, he was making fun of Black people. I told him there were other Dr. Seuss books where he made fun of Asian people with his drawings and his words.

As I told my son that's why we wouldn't be keeping our copy of *The Cat in the Hat*, he said he understood. Weeks later, he did push back on me a bit, telling me that he really wanted to watch the PBS cartoon inspired by the book. I reminded him that it wasn't ok to make fun of Black people for being Black, and that's what Dr. Seuss' Cat character was doing.

This is certainly not the only way I could have handled this situation. Perhaps we could have kept the book since I had explained to my son what was wrong with it. **What was important to me is that I shared with him, in a simple way, what I had learned about racist stereotypes.**

I could have just snuck the book out of his library without another word. But he wouldn't have learned what was problematic about it. He also wouldn't have seen that adults make mistakes, including racist mistakes. I hope that I provided him with an example of one way we can learn and grow after we've participated in racism.

Seeking out racially diverse childcare and playgroups

Diversifying our lives requires more long-term, intentional work than diversifying our bookshelves or toy boxes. But providing children the chance to develop significant cross-racial relationships will also have a bigger impact on reducing prejudice than only diversifying our books and toys.

As parents consider childcare centers and preschools, it's important to ask about the diversity of the student body, as well as how many teachers and staff are people of color.

When my son was a toddler, I was a stay-at-home mom. Living in a segregated city, finding racially diverse playgroups wasn't easy. I ended up choosing one where almost all the kids were white, because I knew several of the moms in the group already.

In hindsight, I wish I'd done more research on Facebook, Meetup, and other sites. We could have spent time playing at parks in predominantly Black or Latinx neighborhoods. We missed opportunities to form relationships with families of color early on in my son's life.

Things to remember

- Toddlers do notice race and want to make sense of what they see.

- Naming skin tone, as well as introducing the racial categories our society uses, helps toddlers label their worlds.

- We can fight the idea that whiteness is normal or standard by making sure that our children's books and toys include kids of many different races, acting in non-stereotypical ways.

- Childcare centers and playgroups that provide toddlers plenty of chances to develop cross-racial friendships are crucial.

Part III
Antiracist parenting in the preschool years

During the preschool years, children are very interested in categorizing people. Maybe you've observed your child talking about how other kids are similar to, or different from, them. Preschoolers sometimes express a strong desire to play with children who they believe are like them.

Because preschoolers don't have complex thinking processes yet, they tend to rely on what they can see as they decide who is like them. They may be very interested in whether or not people "match," asking questions about a parent and child who aren't the same race.

Preschoolers are also curious about what parts of their identities will stay the same and what parts of them will change. They may wonder if they can change their skin color.

All of this means that preschoolers provide us with many opportunities to talk about race.

Helping preschool children learn appropriate labels

Many white parents are hesitant to introduce young children to the racial and ethnic labels that our culture uses. Even parents who talk openly about skin tones, such as peach, tan, and dark brown, often don't use the words Black and white with their children.

It's important to introduce these racial labels too. Why? In the United States, race isn't just about skin color. It's also about culture and history. That's one reason I taught my child the word Black at a young age.

I knew as he grew up, he would hear many white people use the word Black with negative connotations. But Black is not a negative word! I can't help him see all the proud and joyful aspects of Black life and culture if we don't use the word.

I also didn't want our son referring to a Black child as "dark skinned." I wanted him to use the same label that child would use. So, over time, we learned both the terms African American and Black.

Thinking about our family's whiteness, I knew that not naming our own race would teach him that only people of color "have" race and that we are "just normal." So, we talked about various skin tones in our family. My son has more of a light tan skin tone, while mine is a pale peach. But following the lead of parents at the blog *Raising Race Conscious Children*, I also taught him that in our culture, we both have "skin we call white."[13]

Introducing proper racial and ethnic labels (including Latino, Asian American, Arab American, and Native American) helped him understand that there are many different cultures and ethnicities.

The first month he was in preschool, my then 3-year-old kept referring to a classmate as "the kid with the black skin." I soon figured out that he was actually talking about a multiracial child whose mother's ancestry is Thai. Talking about this was perhaps the first time he realized that not everyone is Black or white.

27

Jennifer Harvey's book *Raising White Kids* provides thoughtful guidance on how parents can help white children name race without implying that everyone who is part of a racial group is the same. She gives the example of riding in the car with her children.

When her kids want to tell her something about a person walking down the street, she might say either "You mean that person with a blue coat on, who has light skin – who looks like she might be white?" or "You mean that person carrying a backpack, who looks like she might be Latina?"[14]

Harvey explains that she is deliberate in using the word "might" to describe the person racially. She also makes sure to use other descriptors (the backpack, for example). She explains that children need to see race, but also not make assumptions about people based on their race.

Responding to preschoolers' questions about race

I've learned something valuable from anti-bias educators who work with young children. When a child asks a question (or makes a statement) about race, it's important to first figure out why the child has said what they did.

For example, when a 3½-year-old asked her teacher, "How do people get their color?" her teacher first asked what she thought. Young Sandra, who enjoys coloring her arms and hands with pens, said "I was wondering about pens."

Her teacher affirmed that she was glad Sandra was

trying to figure out this complicated question. She told her that "we get our skin color from our birth mommies and daddies."[15]

This process of showing interest in children's ideas, and then providing simple factual information encourages children to continue talking to us about race.

If we show discomfort or try to avoid answering their questions, children soon learn that race is a shameful topic. They may continue to talk to their peers about their ideas, who won't be able to correct inaccurate information.

When kids internalize racist messages

Society is full of subtle and overt racialized messages about who is beautiful, trustworthy, educated, and hard-working. It can surprise adults when children pick up on these messages and express prejudice.

I'll never forget the gut punch I felt when my 5-year-old saw a Black man getting into his truck and said to me, "I wonder if he stole that car." I can't be sure what informed this racist stereotype, but I suspect having the local tv news on at home, which frequently has racist crime reporting, could have been a factor.

Racist messaging is everywhere, and there's no way caregivers and educators can completely shield children from these messages.

We can, however, be prepared to respond when children do express prejudice. We can also be proactive by surrounding children with messages that challenge the racial stereotypes and racist images they'll encounter elsewhere.

For example, when working on an art project, we can provide materials that reflect a variety of skin tones. This reminds white children that their ethnicity is one of many, rather than being the norm.

As a religious educator, I've seen how doing this can lead to spontaneous conversations about race. One Sunday leading up to Christmas, our church's preschool class was making angels. All the children in the class were white.

We'd read a Bible story about the angel speaking to Mary, and then we made paper plate angels. I provided children with several different colors of construction paper to make the angel's face.

One 5-year-old looked at my sample, which was made with dark brown construction paper. He remarked "My angel looks like the one in the story." The angel in the children's Bible was white, with very pale skin.

"It does look like the one in the story," I responded. "But no one was there to take a picture of the angel, so we don't really know what color their skin was." He nodded and told me that my angel looked like a friend of his from school.

This conversation also prompted me to act on some discomfort I'd been feeling about the images in the curriculum we were using.

I'd noticed a pattern that "heroes" of the Bible stories, like Jesus, the angels, and King David, had very pale skin. Many of the characters kids tend to see as "bad guys" had dark skin. After writing the company, the publisher told me that others had also complained, and they would be re-designing the art in the curriculum.

Setting firm boundaries about rejection and teasing

Ideally, antiracist parents are proactive in talking about being friends with people of all races. We can use stories and everyday conversations to let our children know that it's not okay to reject someone because of their race or other aspects of their identity. But sometimes, we're caught off guard by our children's comments or what a teacher reports to us about our children.

If the teacher calls to tell you that your child made a hurtful comment about race, know that you're not alone.

If that happens, your first reaction may be embarrassment or shame. That's not surprising, but it's important not to pass on that shame to kids. Getting stuck in shame keeps us from being able to effectively show children why what they did was wrong.

.

If the teacher calls

Imagine the teacher informs you that your child told his classmate Eric, "You can't play with us because you've got dark skin"? What should you do?

- Listen carefully and ask questions of the teacher to make sure you understand what happened.

- Take the time you need to calm yourself before talking to your child, whether you find that calm through breathing, meditation, or taking a short walk.

- Without emotion, explain to your child what the teacher described. Set a firm limit: tell your child that it's never okay to tease someone or refuse to play with them because of the things that make them who they are. Be sure to be specific: this means things like their skin color, their language, their gender, a disability, etc.

- Try to figure out whether anything else could be behind your child's behavior. Is he feeling genuinely uncomfortable or anxious? Is he reflecting racism he's heard another adult express? Did he want to only play with his best friend, and inappropriately used race as a reason to exclude Eric? The more you understand what your child may be thinking or feeling, the better you can guide the conversation.

- Reach out to Eric's parents, rather than waiting for them to contact you. Ask if they'd be willing to talk with you about what happened. If you get their consent, apologize directly and tell them what you plan to do to help your child understand why his actions were wrong. Ask Eric's parents if they have thoughts about what else they would like you or your child to do (but don't expect them to solve this problem for you.)

- Remember that whatever you're feeling, Eric's parents are feeling even more hurt for their child. Listen to what they have to say without interrupting. Repeatedly expressing your dismay and shame about what your child did will burden Eric's parents with the task of making you feel better. Instead, reach out to a white friend who shares your commitment to antiracism to unpack how you're feeling.

Why shame doesn't belong in your antiracist toolbox

Parents and caregivers must firmly step in each and every time we see a child expressing racial bias. Ignoring comments or patterns of behavior just gives children permission to repeat their biased behavior, causing lasting harm to other children.

However, shaming children (intentionally or unintentionally) is not helpful in guiding them toward antiracism. Shame emotionally shuts down people of all ages. It disconnects children from themselves and from other relationships.

As a parent, I've felt angry when my child has reflected society's racism. But my anger is best directed at racism, not at my child. My child needs my firm and compassionate guidance so that I can help him unlearn that racism.

Using a calm tone keeps the conversation with our children open. Fussing at or shaming a child who's expressed racism can backfire. Our children will focus on defending themselves, instead of being able to hear what we have to say. They won't be able to reflect on how their words and behaviors hurt someone. They won't think about what they could do differently next time.

When my child expresses bias and I feel a desire to shame him, I try to pause for a moment and look inward. Often, I find that my desire to shame him is as much about my past actions as it is about his current ones. I'll remember when I stayed silent in the face of other people's racism, or when I perpetuated racism and didn't try to make amends later.

Effective action against racism comes from a willingness to learn and be responsible for our actions, not from a place of shame.

Pause and Reflect

Use the worksheet in my free *Raising Antiracist Kids* bonus pack to reflect on your own childhood experiences that could be prompting feelings of shame. Download the pack at antiracistkids.com.

Responding To Racial Bias With Roleplays

Anti-bias educators Louise Derman-Sparks and Julie Olsen Edwards emphasize that when preschool age children express bias and misconceptions, it is often "pre-prejudice." Young children are trying to understand messages they've received (covertly or overtly), but their beliefs haven't necessarily hardened into prejudice yet.

One tool for addressing racial bias that many early childhood educators recommend is roleplays. These can be done proactively before there has been an incident of racism, or in response to something biased a child has already said.

Roleplays are not a substitute for talking directly with a child about their words, especially if they hurt another child. They're simply an additional tool.

Roleplays are easy to do at home if your child has several dolls. If you don't (or a roleplay seems too formal to you), there are other options. Look for a children's book that addresses a stereotype that you think your child struggles with. You can also engage in a wondering time with your child about something they've said.

If a child has made fun of someone speaking another language, for example, you could wonder aloud with them. "I think if someone made fun of how I spoke, I would feel sad or maybe even mad," you might say. "I think my language is beautiful, and I want other people to think it's beautiful too."

Teaching young kids about race, hair, and consent

Many parents know the importance of talking about consent with our children. Perhaps you already tell your children that no one is allowed to touch their body if they don't want them to. You may even risk hurting grandma's feelings by telling your child they don't have to give hugs to family members.

One example of consent that many white children

(and adults) have not thought enough about is touching a Black person's hair. Many Black girls, especially in majority white classrooms, have to endure the microaggression of people touching their hair without permission.

Children are understandably curious about differences between their own hair texture and other children's hair. But we must teach our kids that it's not okay to touch someone's hair without permission. We can also explain to white children why even asking a Black classmate if they can touch her hair could make her feel uncomfortable and singled out.

Reading the picture book *Don't Touch My Hair* by Sharee Miller is a great way to introduce white children to this idea.

Pointing out unfairness and racism

While 4 and 5-year-olds aren't yet ready to handle the more complex information about racism we can share with older kids, they do have a strong sense of fairness! As you go through your daily life together, whether at home or in the classroom, adults can practice noticing what is unfair.

The blog *Raising Race Conscious Children* has many examples of these kinds of "noticing" conversations between children and their parents.

When Shannon Cofrin Gaggero was reading her 5-year-old's favorite magazine to him, she noted out loud that all the children in the magazine were white. Her son remarked that the kids in the magazine had the same kind of skin he did. Gaggero said she wished the magazine had kids with lots of different skin colors, because not everyone is white. Her son responded, "it's not fair to leave anyone out!"

Gaggero points out bias to her children on a regular basis, which is likely why her son was able to make the connection to fairness.[16]

Another step in noticing what's unfair is pointing out people who are working to challenge racism and make things fairer. One of my favorite examples to share with younger kids is Marley Dias.

Marley started the #1000BlackGirlBooks campaign at age 11 because she was tired of never getting to read books starring Black girls at school. So, she started a donation drive, asking people to donate books with Black girl characters. She distributed the books in her community and in Jamaica. Because of her campaign, Marley's school also changed their required reading list.

Noticing what's unfair—and the people who are working to make things fair—prepares young children to have more complex conversations about racism when they're older.

Practice: Help me solve this problem

Ask your child if you can tell them a story. Let them know it includes a problem that you hope they can help you solve.

On the first day of kindergarten, Jessica and Jesus were excited and a little nervous. Over the summer, Jesus spent lots of time playing soccer with his big sister and building block towers. Jessica spent lots of time swimming at the pool and painting.

Both Jesus and Jessica were going to a new school this year because they were starting kindergarten. Jessica knew a lot of the kids from preschool. Jesus didn't know anyone because his family had moved to a new neighborhood over the summer.

On the school bus, Jessica sat next to Jesus. Jesus hugged his backpack in his lap. Jessica was learning to read, so she asked Jesus, "why does it say Jesus (Gee-Zus) on your backpack?"

Jesus told her, "it doesn't say Gee-Zus. It says my name: hay-SOOS. That's how you say my name in Spanish."

Jessica replied, "Well, at my church they taught me that that word is Gee-Zus. That's so funny that your name is Gee-Zus. I'm going to tell everyone I sat next to Gee-Zus on the bus today! Ha! Ha! Ha!"

Jesus got mad and said, "My name is hay-SOOS!" but Jessica didn't listen.

Ask your child what is happening in the story. Help them identify the teasing as not just meanness, but also as racism because the teasing is about Jesus' Latino culture.

What do you think Jesus should do? What could you do if you were riding the bus? What should Jessica do?

Should you introduce 4 and 5-year-olds to the word racism?

We've already talked about how we can help children notice race-related situations that are unfair. As you practice doing this, you might wonder whether to use the word racism.

Isn't it enough to talk about treating everyone fairly?

As parents, we often think that general messages are best. We want our children to be kind all the time. We want them to respect everyone. So, we tell them things like "everybody's equal." We think that we're being clear, but these messages are too vague for concrete-thinking 4 and 5-year-olds to grasp.

For examples, the authors of *NurtureShock* talk about a friend who told her 5-year-old, "remember everybody's equal," repeatedly. After 7 months of this kind of talk, her son looked at her and asked, "what does equal mean?" Talking explicitly about race and racism is a far more effective strategy than telling children that "everyone is equal."

Jennifer Harvey points out that many well-intentioned white adults say this because we <u>want</u> everyone to be treated equally, and we believe everyone <u>should</u> be treated equally. We hope telling our kids this will make them treat others fairly.

While we can tell our children that this is our hope for our community, in the same breath we must tell them that everyone is <u>not yet</u> treated equally.[17] Otherwise, we're training children to ignore racism and prejudice.

We don't need to sit a 4 or 5-year-old down and give them an extended, formal lesson on racism. **But we also shouldn't be afraid to use the word racism when it applies to a situation.**

When we talk to preschool age children about racism, it's best to keep our conversation and examples focused on the present rather than the past. That's because children this age can't distinguish between the recent past (yesterday) and the long ago past (150 years ago). This means that in-depth conversations about how racism worked in the past, such as enslavement, can be confusing to very young children.

Keeping our conversations with preschoolers mostly focused on the present also keeps us from offering narratives that are too tidy, such as "There used to be something called segregation, but brave people worked to end that. Now things are fair."

When we explain what racism is to children, we can add levels of complexity as they get older. I provide more nuanced examples of how to answer the question "what's racism?" in parts IV and V.

For preschoolers, we can keep things simple. Racism is treating someone unfairly because of the color of their skin or their race.

Here are a few examples of racism that preschoolers can understand:

- There are still many children's books that are about a big group of people, like a community or a school, with all white characters. We can ask preschool children, "Do the people in this book look like all the people you know? Who else needs to be included?" This could lead to a conversation about Marley Dias' #1000BlackGirlBooks campaign.

- Too often, white people don't take the time to learn how to say someone's name correctly because its "too hard." We can remind young children that the sounds and names that we are used to sound normal to us, but to someone from another culture, they might sound unusual. We can ask, "How do you feel when people know your name and say it the right way?"

  Though it's a bit long for most 4-year-olds, *The Name Jar* by Yangsook Choi is a great conversation starter for kids ages kindergarten or older.

- The bandages available in stores typically come in only one shade, designed to match white people's skin tone.

  One of my blog readers, Erin F., pointed this out to her 2½-year-old. He immediately said, "We need to make band-aids and color them with other shades." Fortunately, there's a company called Tru-Colour Bandages that already does that. Kids who want to make sure that everyone at their school can have a bandage that matches their skin could donate a box to their classroom.

Whenever possible, caregivers should use the word racism with children as a descriptor, rather than as an insult that implies someone is a horrible person. This lessens some of the emotional punch that we've attached to the word. It might not sound like it at first, but that's actually a good thing.

Labelling something as racism helps us accurately describe what is happening in a situation. That allows us to explore how we can repair the harm caused by the racist act, rather than getting defensive about whether we are racist or not.

Talking to young children about microaggressions

Preschoolers are not too young to learn about microaggressions. It's important that we distinguish between general unkindness and the additional pain that comes from a microaggression.

Whether you use the big word "microaggression" or not is up to you. Sometimes young children are very proud when they can learn to say a long word.

If you're not familiar with the term yourself, psychologist Dr. Derald Wing Sue describes microaggressions as:

> ...the everyday verbal, nonverbal, and environmental slights, snubs, or insults, whether intentional or unintentional, which communicate hostile, derogatory, or negative messages to target persons based solely upon their marginalized group membership.

Because these insults and slights occur on a regular basis, some antiracist educators describe them as "paper cuts" or "mosquito bites." One slight by itself might only be an annoyance, but all the slights combined become a major source of pain and trauma.

Here are a few examples of microaggressions children of color experience:

- Joseph tells his classmate Brittany he is Cherokee. Brittany lets out a war whoop and begins doing the tomahawk chop.

- On the first day of school, Aiden hears his classmate Mei speaking Japanese with her mother.

Aiden laughs and asks, "Why are they talking so funny?"

- Ebony heads for the block area, where Lisa tells her "only people with light skin can play with the blocks."

So, how do we talk about microaggressions to young children? First, we can talk about the different things that make up our identities, the things that make us who we are. Race is one of these, as well as gender, our physical abilities, and our sexual orientation (which I describe as "who we love" to young children.)

Like all conversations with young kids, you'll need to have this one several times before it sinks in. You can talk about real life examples of people you know, as well as draw from children's books and media.

Once we've established what "identity" is, we can let children know that it's very hurtful to tease or exclude someone because of their identity. This might be the conversation where you teach the big word microaggression. You could describe it as "hurtful things people say or do that are about who someone is—their identity."

This is also a good place to teach children that even if we didn't <u>intend</u> to hurt someone's feelings (which is the case with many microaggressions), what matters is that we <u>did</u> hurt them.

We can practice how to apologize after we've committed a microaggression. Parents can help kids brainstorm what they could say if they see someone else insult a person's identity. This could include teaching kids the phrase, "it's not ok to tease someone because of who they are."

Finally, I appreciate what first grader teacher Bret

43

Turner tells his students. He lets them know that while it might hurt your feelings for someone to tell you something you said is racist, it hurts much, much more to be the one who's on the receiving end of racism.

What do we say about racism and violence?

Racism is closely tied with violence. With young children, it can be hard to know whether we should discuss examples of racism that include violence.

Violence and death are more frightening to young children than they are in the elementary years (though these are never easy topics.) That's led many educators of young children, including those who have an antiracism focus, to steer clear of topics about violence.

For example, kindergarten teacher Laleña Garcia, who is a leader in the Black Lives Matter at School movement, shares how she talks about Black Lives Matter to her students.

She describes the movement to her young students as:

> ...a group of people who want to make sure that everyone is treated fairly, regardless of the color of their skin. We can say something along the lines of "The Civil Rights Movement, with people we know about, like Martin Luther King, Jr. and Rosa Parks, worked to change laws that are unfair. The Black Lives Matter movement is made up of people who want to make sure that everyone is treated fairly, because, even though many of those laws were changed many years ago, some people are still

44

not being treated fairly."

Garcia says that just as she doesn't discuss the violence that met civil rights activists with her 5-year-old class, neither does she introduce topics about present day police violence.[18]

But I also know that the conversations a parent has are different than ones that take place at school.

When we talk about tough topics one-on-one with our kids, parents can monitor how they're reacting. We can ask them questions to see what they understand. Parents can respond to our children's fears in a way that's difficult for a teacher to do in a large group.

As the parent of a white child, I'm also aware that it's very easy for me to avoid discussions that make me uncomfortable in the name of protecting my child's innocence. Knowing that, I decided around the age of 4 to let our son know that Black and white people in our city were often treated very differently by the police.

Without going much detail, I told him that many Black people don't feel safe around the police. I shared that police officers are more likely to pull over cars with Black drivers and more likely to arrest Black people, even when they haven't done anything wrong.

A year later, when the picture book *Something Happened In Our Town* was published, it helped me continue the conversation in a more structured way. The story describes a Black family and white family's reactions to the shooting of an unarmed Black teen in their community.

As parents of white kids, we have to figure out a delicate balance.

Many Black, Latinx, and Native American parents

have to talk to their kids about the realities of police violence at young ages. They face the burden of knowing that the survival strategies they share with their kids will likely increase their children's stress and fear. Parents of color can't opt out of these conversations, so I feel I shouldn't avoid them either.

At the same time, I'm relying on psychologists and educators, both white and people of color, who caution against sharing too much detail with young children.

When our son was 4-years- old, I took him to the National Civil Rights Museum. As we went through the museum, I spent too much time emphasizing that some civil rights leaders were killed. My son became withdrawn and asked to go home. I didn't keep our conversation age appropriate, and he shut down emotionally.

As I reflect on the conversations we've had, I can think of times I shared too much. But there are other times that I gave into my own discomfort too quickly and avoided talks that should have happened.

While I've never guided these conversations perfectly, I do know that my son is much better off for having had these conversations about racism than if we hadn't attempted them at all.

Providing white children opportunities to be resilient

One of the greatest obstacles that keeps white adults from doing antiracist work is what Robin Di'Angelo describes as "white fragility." Here's how Di'Angelo explains the concept:

White people in North America live in a social

environment that protects and insulates them from race-based stress. This insulated environment of racial protection builds white expectations for racial comfort while at the same time lowering the ability to tolerate racial stress, leading to what I refer to as white fragility. White Fragility is a state in which even a minimum amount of racial stress becomes intolerable, triggering a range of defensive moves."[19]

What does this have to do with raising kids who want to do the work of antiracism? Two things. First, our own white fragility as parents often leads to exaggerated fears about our children experiencing racially stress.

Let me give an example from my own life that is painful for me to admit. When our son was 3 years old, he started attending a small, private, and predominantly white Montessori school. It was a wonderful school in almost every way except its racial makeup.

As he got a bit older and could have attended public school, I began to have misgivings. As the daughter of a public school teacher and a product of public schools myself, I felt uncomfortable that I was opting out of public schools. I also knew that the racial makeup of his private school was allowing him to exist in a white racial bubble, while living in a majority Black city.

When our son was 4, I heard from a few other moms in an online Facebook group about how happy they were with a new charter Montessori school in our city. It was located in a majority Black, working class neighborhood, although a small minority of white families from other neighborhoods also enrolled their kids there.

I thought about taking a look at the school. But I didn't even go visit. Why?

Though I gave myself a lot of other reasons, the truth is that fear kept me from visiting. I let my racist stereotypes about Black boys guide my decision. I imagined whether my gentle, introverted, white son would fit in at the school and assumed he wouldn't be able to handle it.

It took me another two years before I faced up to the racism inside me, visited the school, and eventually enrolled him.

That brings me to my second point about white fragility and children. When parents shelter our white children from experiences that we fear will be stressful, such as being in majority Black settings, we pass on our fragility to them.

In the weeks before class started at his new school, our son expressed worries that he might be the only white child in his class. Once school started, he also made some assumptions about his Black classmates based on their race.

The flip side of this is that it only took him a couple of weeks of attending a majority Black school for him to become more resilient. His experiences in his new class showed him that he didn't have to be in the racial majority to feel comfortable.

Unlike many white adults in our city who will go to great lengths to avoid being in the racial minority even for a brief period of time, our son now sees that this situation doesn't have to be stressful.

Here are some other ways we can help white children let go of fragility and become more resilient:

- Gently but firmly pointing out when something a child has done is based on a racial stereotype or is hurtful to a person of color. We must name race in

48

this situation, rather than just talking about being unkind.

- Model apologizing and doing what we can to make amends after we've said or done something racist. Also, when we catch ourselves reflecting a racial stereotype in front of our children, we need to stop and explain what was wrong with our thinking.

- Making a commitment to spend more time in places where white people are not the majority. (This assumes that the event or group you're joining welcomes your presence. Read event descriptions to make sure they're not specified for people of color only.) We can think about where we worship, the cultural events we attend, the circles we socialize in, the parks we play in, and even the schools our children attend and neighborhoods we live in. Where can we take a first step? As we become more comfortable in spaces that were once unfamiliar or even stressful, our children will notice the difference and benefit from the cross-racial relationships we're developing.

What if our kids are thankful for their white privilege?

It's not surprising that learning about the realities of racism will sometimes lead white children to be glad they don't have to experience these injustices. But it's still unsettling when our kids articulate that gratitude.

When my youngest son was 5 years old, President Trump was threatening to take away DACA protections for immigrant young adults. I was distraught, especially thinking of two young DREAMers I knew.

I read the book *Mama's Nightingale* to our son, which tells the story of a Haitian-American child whose mother is in immigration detention. We talked about how unfair it is that the government can take parents away from their children, just because they don't have "the right papers."

My son asked to read the story several more times in the coming days. Most nights that we read the book, he would look at me and ask, "But we have the right papers, don't we, Mama?" I knew he wanted my reassurance that we wouldn't be separated, which I gave him. But I couldn't let that reassurance be the end of our conversation.

I told him that I believed that every family deserved to be able to live together and to feel safe. "So, I'm glad we have the right papers, but I'm very sad that many people don't. And that's why it's so important to me that we speak up with people who don't have the right papers. Because every kid wants and needs to be with their family, right?"

Helping young children take action

Developmentally, 4 and 5-year-olds are very tuned into themselves and their immediate surroundings. So, as we talk with young children about racism, the examples they're most likely to resonate with are the ones that touch their lives.

One of the ways we can support young children's antiracist journeys is to ask them what they'd like to do when they notice something is unfair.

For example, Nancy Spangler's 3 and 4-year-old class was a place where teachers and students worked hard to make everyone feel included. But one day when she pulled out a game, Ms. Spangler noticed that all the characters in the game were white.

She drew the children's attention to this and asked them if the cards "look like all the people you know?" The children said no, identifying many kinds of people who were missing from the card set.

Ms. Spangler helped the children draft a letter to the maker of the cards. The children also used skin tone pens they already had in the classroom to re-color the cards so they would "look real."[20]

Sometimes, young children can also take action in ways that go beyond their immediate surroundings.

After my son and I read the book *Mama's Nightingale* and talked about families being separated, I decided to write letters to our Senators. I urged them to support the DACA program, and also keep families together.

I asked my son if he'd like to write a sentence to add to the letter, which he did. This also gave us an opportunity to talk about how laws are made, and how important it is to speak up to the people who make our laws.

We can also keep antiracist action in the forefront of children's minds by talking about what we're doing as adults.

One night, my son alarmed me by singing a song in the shower that included the word "r*dskin."

I found out a teacher's assistant had been reading the book *Peter Pan* to his class, a book that has terrible stereotypes about Native Americans and includes a made-up tribe name that's also a slur for Black people.

I spoke with his teacher about the book. Since an assistant had been reading the story, the teacher didn't even remember the racist content in *Peter Pan*, thinking of it only as a "classic book."

I encouraged her to talk to the children about the stereotypes in the book, since they'd already read it. I pointed out that in our part of the country we often give racist stereotypes about indigenous people a "pass" because they are so few Native Americans in our community. She agreed that it was a problem.

While I didn't tell my son every detail of our conversation, I let him know that I'd talked with his teacher and why. I want the adults in his life to model a pattern for him: when we notice racism, we speak up.

Things to remember

- When young children make biased remarks or ask questions about race, it's important to ask for their thoughts first.

- As parents, we must set firm limits for children that it's not okay to reject someone based on their identity.

- Shaming children for saying something racist can make them defensive, hampering our efforts to raise antiracist kids.

- Preschool age children can learn the names for races that our culture uses, showing them that it's okay to talk about race.

- Vague statements about treating everyone fairly won't help young children understand how to spot racism or speak up against it.

- White children need opportunities that help them become resilient in the face of racial stress, such as not being in the racial majority all the time.

- As kids learn about racism, they may say they're glad they're white. We can share how we want people of color to feel safe in the same ways that we already do as white people.

53

Part IV
Antiracist parenting in the elementary years

In the elementary years, children's ability to reason and understand complex ideas grows by leaps and bounds. This developmental change means that parents and caregivers can talk at a more in-depth level about how race affects our lives. We can help children look at the larger impact racism has on society today and has had in the past.

It's important at every developmental stage to have open, on-going conversations about race with kids. But there's one research study about white kids in the elementary years that caught my attention (and truthfully alarmed me a bit!)

Researchers gave white children ages 5 to 10 pictures of Black children and white children. They asked children to allocate resources to each child who was pictured.

The 5 to 7-year-old children discriminated against Black children in how they distributed the resources, regardless of whether they were alone, or a Black woman researcher was present.

The 8 to 10-year-olds also discriminated, but they were less likely to do so when a Black woman researcher was in the room with them.

In other words, the older children were learning to hide their racism depending on who was watching them.[21]

Our children need to hear directly from us that racial discrimination is wrong. Even more importantly, they need to see us putting this principle into action.

Do you need to do catch up work?

There are many perceptive researchers and writers who've written about children's racial development. As humans, we develop physically, emotionally, and mentally. Racial identity development theory, pioneered by Dr. Janet Helms, recognizes that we also develop racially.

I'll share more about the stages of racial identity development in part VI. For now, what's important to know is that a **child's age doesn't necessarily tell us where they are in the racial development process.** That's especially true for children who haven't had regular, healthy conversations about race with adults.

So, if your child is between the ages of 6–11 and you're just starting to talk to them about race, you may have some "catch-up work" to do.

That's ok. You can only start where you are now. The important thing is that you've committed to antiracism in your parenting. I encourage you to skim parts II and III about toddlers and preschoolers. You'll find several ideas for conversation and action that you can modify to fit your child at the age they are right now.

Creating opportunities for cross-racial relationships

The authors of *NurtureShock: New Thinking about Children*, share research suggesting the early elementary years may be a critical window for challenging white children's racial bias.

For example, one study required children to complete school projects in cross racial groups over an eight-week period. The researchers found that this classwork significantly increased cross racial friendships on the playground for first graders.

By the third grade, however, this intervention made no difference in who played together.[22]

Around the time that our youngest son turned 6, I started thinking much more intensely about his friendships, almost all of which were with white children. This especially troubled me because our family lives in a majority Black city. Our community also has smaller but significant Latinx and Asian American populations. It's a community where children's lives are, for the most part, highly segregated.

Once my son was born, my life mostly followed that segregated pattern. My stepson (now a college student) attended majority Black middle and high schools, yet most of his social circle was white. Our church, where we spend a lot of time, is predominantly white with a handful of Black members.

Since I'd left my community organizing job to become a stay at home parent, I'd lost the regular interactions I'd had with Black and Latinx colleagues. At the time, my son's school was almost entirely white.

My husband and I talked with our son about race often, starting when he was preschool age. We read and discussed many books about racism and the brave people who had taken antiracist action. I took him to a rally for immigrant children and talked about why we were there. We talked about police violence and Black Lives Matter.

As I shared earlier, we decided to enroll our younger son in a majority Black public Montessori school in second grade. Because of all our conversations about race, I hoped he would be prepared.

My husband and I talked with him about how we were glad he would be attending a school with more Black children, because that's what our city looks like. I told him that I think we learn better when we learn alongside people from different backgrounds.

He seemed to understand this. But the week before school started, he kept asking questions that showed he was worried about the racial makeup of the school.

Would there be other white kids like him? Would he make friends? He brightened up a bit when I told him that his new school was a lot like the elementary school I attended, and that I had both Black and white friends at his age.

When I picked him up on the first day of school, he told me the day had been "some good, some bad." The bad part was that one kid, a Black kid, kept touching him. And he was feeling nervous because most of the other kids in his class were Black. He seemed uncertain that any of them could become a friend.

From what he described, it sounded like the other child was trying to be playful with him. I told our kiddo he could say in a kind but firm way "I don't like to be touched. Please don't do that." I also reminded him of two white classmates from his old school who were often physical with him in their play, which my son didn't like.

"So, I think all we know about the person who touched you at your new school is that it's hard for him to keep his hands to himself," I said. "It's not because he's Black. Someone's race doesn't tell us everything about who they are."

He looked at me somewhat doubtfully, but he didn't say anything else. I mentally held my breath for the next couple of days. I wondered how things could have been different if we'd sought out a more diverse school when he started kindergarten, but I tried not to stress about the past.

Each day as our son met new people (kids and adults) he told me about them and always pointed out what their races were. By week-two of school, he'd told me that he'd made four friends: two were white and two were Black. In the space of a few days, being in a multiracial classroom was starting to reduce his prejudices and anxieties.

We still have a lot more work to do, as adults and with our younger child, to desegregate our lives beyond school and strengthen our commitment to antiracism. But the experience of choosing a new school showed me something important.

All the conversation in the world can't substitute for real relationships with kids of color.

Practice: Evaluate your children's book collection

In part II, I talked about the value of diverse books for toddlers. As children grow older, they usually play a bigger role in selecting their own books. That's why the elementary years are a great time for your kids to help you determine how diverse your home library actually is.

Each year, the Cooperative Children's Book Center at the University of Wisconsin counts how many new children's books published that year have lead characters that are African American, Native American, Latinx, and Asian, as well as how many were written by authors of color.

While the number of children's books by and about people of color has been increasing in the past few years, it's far from representing the actual racial makeup of the United States.

Before taking a look at your book collection, ask your child a few questions, such as:

- How easy is it for you to find books that have characters who are white? (You could also add books with families that are similar to our family, books where kids live in a house that's a lot like ours, etc.)

- How do you think you would feel if it was really hard to find books at your school, the library, or the bookstore where the characters were white?

Invite your child to make a bit of a mess by pulling their books off the shelf one at a time. Make one pile of books for books with animal and non-human characters. Separate the remaining books into piles based on the main character's race.

After you've made your piles, if your child is interested in math, you could figure out the percentages of your book collection that are in each pile. You could compare these percentages to the racial makeup of the U.S. population. For example, the Census reports that Black people make up about 13% of U.S. residents. What percentage of your books have Black main characters?

Here are a few other ideas for discussion:

- Start a conversation about representation by checking whether the authors share the race of the main character. (The author's bio will usually give you clues to this.) Why does that matter?

- Do any of the books reflect stereotypes about how a particular racial group thinks, acts, or lives? One stereotype that's common is only showing Native American characters as they lived in the past, not the present.

- Are there any books that lump large groups together, making it seem like a single culture? For example, many children's books are set in "Africa," an enormous and diverse continent, rather than in a particular country in Africa.

Ask your child if they notice any racial group that is underrepresented in your home library. Find ideas for new books to add to your library in the resources section at the end of the book.

Talking about whether race is real

There have been many people in U.S. history who've used eugenics to spread racist ideas. They've claimed that there are essential, biological differences in intelligence based on what "race" a person belongs to.

While many white liberals assumed this talk was a thing of the past, openly white supremacist ideas are on the rise, both online and in the public square.

It's important to let children know that race is not real in the biological sense. Children notice physical characteristics like hair texture and skin tone. They see that the shapes of eyes, noses, and lips sometimes differ among people of different races.

Some children may believe that these surface level physical traits mean that people belonging to different racial groups are fundamentally different from each other in a biological sense.

We can tell children that when people talk about race today, most often they're referring to where a person's ancestors came from. We can tell kids that scientists who study genetics have found that there's no genetic combination that makes a person Arab, Asian, white, Black, or Latinx.

For example, they've found that there's more diversity between people who live within Africa than there is between Africans and non-Africans.[23]

But in the same conversation that we teach children that race isn't real in the biological sense, we need to immediately follow with a second idea. **Race is a very real concept in the social sense.**

Because society has decided that race matters, it makes a huge difference in our life experiences. For one, race has become one of the significant ways that cultures are celebrated and passed on. Secondly, as we discuss frequently in this book, race affects our access to resources, our experiences of discrimination or privilege, and even our mental and physical health.

You've probably heard a well-meaning adult tell children "race doesn't matter." Sometimes they're trying to get kids to understand that biological race isn't real. They may also want kids to understand that race shouldn't be an impediment to making friendships and working together.

But race does matter. Telling white children that race doesn't matter encourages them to believe the colorblind lie that everyone already competes on a level playing field.

As Ijeoma Oluo wrote in her accessible guide *So You Want to Talk about Race*, the fact that race is a social construct doesn't lessen its impact:

> *Money is also a social construct—a series of rules and agreements we all made up while pretending that these pieces of paper are worth our entire*

lives. But we cannot simply stop thinking of money and it will cease to enthrall us. It has woven its way into every part of our lives. It has shaped our past and our futures. It has become alive.[24]

White children need to know how race matters, to their life experiences and to those of children of color.

Talking about history and heroes

Unlike the preschool years, elementary age children can easily understand the difference between the past and the present. That means we can talk more about how race has impacted history. In turn, that helps kids make sense of how race affects the present.

Younger elementary children are likely to see historical figures as primarily heroes or villains. As antiracist parents, we need to talk to our kids about how history is complicated. Many of the same people our children have been told are heroes also upheld racism in both their private and public lives.

In the fall of 2019, I was quoted in an article from *The Washington Post* on talking to children about slavery. I posted the article on social media. The very next day, a friend told me that she was so glad she'd read the advice from educators in the article, because her 8-year-old had come rushing into the room distressed, holding a book in his hand. "Mama, this says George Washington and Thomas Jefferson owned slaves!" he told her. "Is that true? I thought they were good guys!"

As Jennifer Harvey writes:

...we teach enslavement. We teach George Washington. But we never connect the two. This is

*very dangerous to our children's sense of history
and to their consciousness overall.*[25]

Telling the truth about historical figures lays an important foundation for children. They must understand how widespread racism has been throughout history and how persistent it is today, so that they can understand why it will take more than personal change to dismantle racism.

Kids also deserve the more truthful, complicated stories about people we hold up as heroes for peace and justice. One example is Mahatma Gandhi. We can teach children about his incredible legacy of nonviolent resistance and what it meant to the people of India. But we should also share that Gandhi used racist slurs when talking about Black South Africans, something that prompted the Ghanaian government to take down a statue of Gandhi in 2018.[26]

Giving children a more accurate picture of history's leaders can show kids that rooting out racism is no simple matter. It reminds kids and adults alike that our work against racism, within ourselves and in society, must be ongoing.

Starting these complicated conversations about history, in the moments when they come up, does something else important.

College professors who teach about race-related topics can tell you that some of their white students are indignant, hostile, or greatly disillusioned when they begin to learn the more complicated truths about racism in the United States.

If parents can begin these conversations with our children now, they won't have to ask many years later "why didn't anyone tell me the truth?"

As we talk about white people in history who've perpetuated racism, it's crucial to emphasize the resistance of people of color. To go back to the example of George Washington, we can tell kids about Ona Judge, who was enslaved by Martha Washington.

When Judge found out that she was going to be given to Martha's granddaughter as a wedding gift, she boldly made her escape. Even when President Washington sent an associate to trick her into returning, Judge refused to give up her freedom, and she was never re-enslaved.

Finally, we need to give our children examples of white allies who have taken risks rather than simply accepting the privileges of being white. This is tricky, because we don't want to exaggerate the number of white people who have been actively antiracist. We also don't want to give kids the simplistic impression that there are "good white people" and "bad white people." But we can tell them about white people who dedicated themselves to antiracist movements, like Joan Trumpauer (featured in the children's book *She Stood for Freedom*) and Anne Braden.

Anne Braden and her husband were charged with sedition in 1954 for helping a black family desegregate their neighborhood in Louisville, Kentucky. (I'm still hoping someone might write a children's book about her.)

Learning more than surface level histories of people of color

Attending majority Black schools in the 1980s and 90s, I learned more about Black history than many of my white peers in other communities. Even so, the way we were taught that history sometimes led to white kids thinking of Black people as victims of a long, sad history.

If we're going to help children learn everyone's history, we need to include truthful stories about oppressive systems like enslavement, Jim Crow segregation, the theft of Native American land, and the internment of Japanese Americans during World War II.

But we also must go beyond teaching about these systems of oppression to include the history that rarely gets told to children.

Do our kids know about the ancient African civilizations whose accomplishments rival that of the Greeks and Romans? For example, many of the concepts that students learn in high school math today were first developed in Egypt 35,000 years ago.[27]

How much do your children know about the indigenous nation(s) whose land your family lives on today?

As a child and a young adult, all I remember learning about the Chickasaw nation is that they were here long ago, and that they were forced to leave so that my city could be founded. I'm frustrated by what I didn't learn, so our family has made an effort to learn as much as we can about Chickasaw history.

Do we talk about the accomplishments of Black, Latinx, Native American, and Asian Americans only during designated months? Do we limit what we learn to what Rethinking Schools calls "heroes and holidays?" Or are we willing to decenter white people as we learn and talk about American history and world history year-round?

Talking with kids about cultural appropriation

Cultural appropriation is a tricky topic, and it's one that more white people need to grapple with. If our children ask if they can wear a Moana costume for Halloween or wear their hair in dreadlocks, is this cultural appropriation?

Before talking with our kids, it's important for adults to understand that cultural appropriation isn't just an exchange between different cultures.

Cultural appropriation always involves a power dynamic. In the United States, that dynamic is white people taking aspects of culture from people of color, without their invitation or permission. Cultural appropriation also often involves white people being able to make money from appropriation by imitating art, jewelry, or clothing and selling it.

So, what can we say if a child asks if she can dress up as Pocahontas for Halloween, or if he can wear his hair in a mohawk? Here are examples of what you can say or ask in your conversation.

- "It's a good thing to appreciate what's beautiful or interesting about someone else's culture. Tell me more about why you want to do ____."

- "What we don't want to do is take from a culture that isn't ours, especially if people from that culture have asked us not to."
- "I wonder if this costume is based on stereotypes about this culture. Do you think this is how someone who is _____ dresses today?"
- "One thing we need to figure out is whether the mohawk you're asking to get has a special meaning. Did you know the name comes from the Mohawk tribe? Let's do some research to find out more."
- "I wonder if parts of this costume are sacred, which means it's related to someone's beliefs about God. I've learned that feathers are sacred to many Native American tribes. So that would mean we shouldn't use them to make a Native American craft."
- "Let's find out who is making these clothes and whether they are part of the culture this style comes from."

For specific examples of how parents have talked to kids of different ages about cultural appropriation (including mohawks and Halloween costumes), see the resources section at the end of

Looking for the resisters

In the summer of 2019, law enforcements officers killed one of my stepson's classmates from high school,

Brandon Webber. I broke the news to our 20-year-old about his classmate, an artist and student leader who'd held so much promise. Then, I thought about what I wanted our 7-year-old to know.

I wanted our younger child to know that Brandon's friends and family and former teachers were gathering to celebrate who he was and to tell the police to stop hurting their neighborhood. I told him about the vigil that his big brother and I attended, and how clergy and churches were calling for an end to police violence against Black and Latinx people in our city.

My goal was for our younger son to know not only that a racist tragedy had happened, but also that people were taking antiracist action.

One of my favorite stories about Mr. Rogers is from his childhood. He says that whenever he would see something scary on the news, "My mother would say to me: 'Look for the helpers. You will always find people who are helping.'"

As our children learn more about the realities of race and racism, we can encourage them to do something similar by "looking for the resisters."

Help your child notice people of color resisting racism in concrete ways in your community and beyond. Point out examples of Latinx, indigenous, Black, and Asian people who've refused to be defined by racist stereotypes and who are celebrating their culture and history. Show them white allies who listen to the voices of activists of color and who amplify their messages in places where other white people often don't want to hear their words.

Each time we do this, we remind our kids that even though racism has a long history, we do not have to accept

69

injustice as inevitable. There will always be people bravely resisting.

Describing racism to elementary age children

In *Raising White Kids*, Jennifer Harvey describes a conversation with one of her daughters about Rosa Parks. In that conversation, **she described racism as "all the beliefs, behaviors, and laws in our society that harm African American people, Latino people, and all people of color."**[28] To it, we can also add that these same beliefs, behaviors, and laws give unfair advantages to white people.

When trying to help children understand what racism is, specific examples help a lot. Here are a few examples of racism that we can ask children if they've noticed:

- Black students are much more likely to receive out-of-school suspensions than white students in situations where their behavior is similar.[29] Ask your child, "Have you ever noticed Black (or Latinx) children getting punished more often at school for doing the same thing that white kids are doing?"

- Most school curriculum, from history to the arts to literature, puts white people at the center. When looking at a history book's chapter on the Civil War, for example, we can ask "whose perspective do you think this history is being told from? How would this event be described if it were told from the perspective of an enslaved person?"

70

- It's very common for native born Asian American people to be asked "where are you from?" or be told things like "your English is so good!" We can ask children, "How do you think it feels to be asked those questions? What are people trying to say when they make remarks like those?"

Teaching children that the word "racist" is not a slur

Imagine for a moment that someone told you that something you said was racist. How do you feel? If you're like most white people, you'd probably think this was one of the worst things someone could say about you.

But antiracism author Ibram Kendi thinks we need to abandon the idea that the word "racist" is a slur. Instead we should think of it as a descriptive term that states what an idea or action is.

Why? Kendi gives several reasons. First, we tend to use the term racist as a fixed identity. We see particular people as racist, and other people as not racist. But racism shapes all of us.

Kendi, who is Black, points to a high school speech he gave honoring Dr. Martin Luther King as an example. Today, he realizes that speech was filled with racist anti-Black ideas, such as complaining that Black youth don't value education. In a moment when he thought he was standing against racism, he was actually proclaiming popular racist ideas.

Second, people throughout American history have denied being racist, from Jim Crow segregationists to white nationalists today. That leads to the question, "if

71

there are no racists, why is there still racism?"

Finally, Dr. Kendi writes, if we understand the word racist as just describing someone in a specific moment, we realize that the same person can be both racist and antiracist. **Most people believe both racist and antiracist ideas.**[30]

This approach is a valuable one when talking to children and teens about racism. When something is labelled racist, we need to stop and evaluate. Instead of getting wrapped up in defending someone with comments like "I know their heart, they aren't racist," we can focus on the particular comment, idea, or action.

Is it a belief or action that hurts people of color and gives white people unfair advantages, whether that harm happened intentionally or not? If yes, then it is racism.

Helping kids understand when prejudice is not racism

Sometimes, when white children attend schools where they are not the racial majority, they experience kids of color excluding them because they are white.

These incidents of prejudice can be hurtful, as I remember from my own childhood. But I believe they're not the same as racism, and it's important for us to talk to our children about the difference between the two.

Take, for example a white child who's feeling hurt after being told by a Black child that he can't join in a playground game. Parents can empathize with the child's hurt and affirm that what happened wasn't fair. It can be helpful to describe what happened as prejudice or judging someone based on their skin color. But a parent shouldn't describe what happened as racism, and if a child does use that word, they need be gently corrected.

We can explain that racism is prejudice that's backed up by patterns of discrimination that go beyond just a few kids on the playground. We can distinguish between the examples of racism shared in this book and what happened to our white child.

When people of color experience racism, it's not just their feelings that get hurt. There are long term consequences to racism that deny resources to people of color, and that give white people unfair advantages in jobs, education, housing, health care, and more.

Model speaking up against racism

Earlier, I mentioned a research study about children learning to hide their racial biases depending on who was in the room with them. Starting at age 8, many kids had already learned to hide their racial bias if a Black woman researcher was in the room, but to behave in biased ways if they were alone.

Children are such perceptive imitators of adults, from close relatives to adults they observe in the media. Children often see white adults engaging in racism or tolerating other people's racist remarks in all white spaces. They learn that racism is commonplace. They get the idea that as long as there are no people of color around whose feelings could get hurt, it's acceptable to say racist things. That's why it's so important that we speak up when family, friends, and acquaintances engage in racist talk.

I know how anxiety-provoking this is. I've used my introversion as an excuse for why I couldn't speak up many times. Other times, I've wanted to speak but felt frozen in shock. For many years, I'd seen few real-life examples of how to speak up well. But I also know that the harm my silence does to people of color, to my impressionable child, and to my soul is too great a cost to bear any longer.

So, how do we speak up? Here are a few ideas:

- Consider whether you're equipped to say something right in the moment, or if it would be better to speak to this person privately.

- Francesca Ramsey of *MTV Decoded* finds that playing dumb in the face of a racist joke can be an effective strategy in certain situations. "I just don't get why that joke is funny. Can you explain it to me?"

- In other situations, Ramsey suggests being more direct, saying something like "I'm just not comfortable with that joke. Please don't say stuff like that around me."

- If you've decided to speak to someone privately, it's likely because you have a relationship with them. The Southern Poverty Law Center's guide *Speak Up!* recommends emphasizing that relationship. You can say something like "I love you so much, and I want to spend time with you. But your comments about Black people are putting distance between us."[31]

- Other relatives may require much more firm limits. One woman featured in *Speak Up!* had a father-in-law who told racist jokes in front of her children. When she arrived at the next family gathering, she told him she knew she couldn't control what he said, but that she found his jokes offensive and wouldn't allow her children to listen to them. She explained that she would be leaving with the children if he made a racist joke. It took three different family visits where she and the children left, but her father-in-law finally stopped his behavior.

- If your follow up conversation was in private but the racist remark was made in front of your children, let your child know that you spoke up.

What if you keep thinking about an opportunity you had to speak up, but you stayed silent? I have relatives who live in a predominantly white suburb of our city. In the past, they've repeatedly made jokes about their safety when they come to visit us in our urban neighborhood. Their remarks usually include coded racist language, rather than being explicit.

My frustration with my own silence has compelled me to make a plan for the next time this happens. I plan to ask them if I can talk to them privately. I'll say something like, "you may feel like you're just making a joke, but it sounds to me you're saying our neighborhood isn't safe because there are Black people here. I love our neighborhood and our family feels safe here. I'm worried your jokes are teaching my child to be afraid of Black people. Please don't say those kinds of things, even as a joke, in front of him."

Of course, it's also important that we tell children when we've been confronted with our own racist biases. Talking honestly about our own racist mistakes contributes to our children's positive racial development.

Realizing that we said or did something racist often brings shame. But talking about what we did with our kids, and what we will do to try to make the situation right, models to them that people can't be permanently categorized as "racist" and "not racist."

Exploring the moving walkway of racism

As we learned from Ibram Kendi in the introduction, "not being racist" isn't enough in our society. We must go beyond neutrality to embrace active antiracism.

Older elementary children can understand a metaphor for racism that psychology professor Beverly Daniel Tatum developed. She asks us to imagine the moving walkway at the airport. The walkway represents how the cycle of systemic racism is maintained.

People who walk quickly down the walkway to get to their gate as fast as possible represent "active racism: blatant, intentional acts of racial bigotry and discrimination." These are the people we first think of when we use the word *racist*, such as the tiki torch waving white supremacists who marched through Charlottesville, Virginia in 2017.

The people who just stand on the walkway and let it slowly take them to their destination represent passive racism, which Tatum describes as less overt. Examples include laughing when a racist joke is told, failing to challenge discriminatory hiring practices, avoiding talk about race, or accepting when people of color are omitted from curriculum.

Those who participate in passive racism probably see themselves as "not racist." They didn't make the joke, or create the curriculum, or initiate the hiring policy. But by not challenging these jokes and policies, they are still carried along the moving walkway.

Both types of people arrive at the destination of racism, just at different speeds.

The only way to not be carried to the destination of racism, Tatum points out, is to actively walk in the opposite direction of the walkway by taking antiracist action.[32]

Jennifer Harvey also uses the metaphor of the moving walkway to help children understand structural racism. She talks with her children about how "structural racism is the thing that built the walkway, put us all on it, and set it running in the particular direction in the first place."

For the walkway to continue working, it must be maintained. Sometimes that happens in ways we can't even see.[33] We can also talk to kids about how individually, we can walk the opposite direction on the walkway to show our opposition to racism. But when work collectively, we can do things that will actually cause the racist walkway to break down.

Strategizing about how to respond to racism

If we've practice noticing race and racism with our children, eventually they will start bringing up examples of racism we haven't even perceived ourselves. How can we support our kids in speaking up and taking action?

First, we must be open to their observations, even when those observations are about us, or about other adults we trust. It's easy to get defensive or talk about what someone's intentions were. Instead, we can ask questions about what our children observed. We can find out if they have any ideas about why this situation is happening.

As parents, we can brainstorm or roleplay with our children about how they want to respond to racist remarks or incidents. We can help them identify other kids who may share their concerns and ask what they could do together.

One day, Cedar Pruitt and her 9-year-old daughter Pearl were heading to the public pool in Newton, Massachusetts. Pearl looked at a mural hanging in the entrance to the pool. She looked up at her mom and said, "Everyone in that mural is white, and that must not be welcoming for all children." Her mother was surprised that she'd never noticed this herself.

Pearl decided to write a letter to the City about the mural, asking them to change it. The Pruitts found out that a local art teacher had also been bothered by the mural and wanted to repaint it. The Pruitts started a GoFundMe campaign, which successfully raised money for supplies so that the mural could be changed.

Teaching kids about antiracism through children's literature

Walking in the opposite direction on the moving walkway of racism sounds like hard work. Any kid who's tried to walk the wrong way on an actual airport walkway will recognize this! So, we need to tell them lots of stories about kids and adults who've done just that.

In the resources section at the end of the book, you'll find a list of children's books about antiracist leaders and the movements they are part of. One of the things that I like to do with these books is emphasize the group action that took place.

In our individualistic society, we tend to only tell the story of the hero, as if that person made change all by themselves. We tell the story of how Rosa Parks refused to move on the bus, but not her prior work with the NAACP or the non-violent resistance training she received at the Highlander Center.

We don't talk about the sacrifices that thousands of Black Birmingham bus riders made for a year while they refused to ride. We forget about the people who organized carpools and mass meetings.

Stories are also a powerful way to show white kids that even though most white people have not engaged in the work of antiracism, it is possible for them to do so.

We need to tell the truth about white people's participation in racism. But if we don't also give our kids examples of white people who've gone against the grain by fighting racism, they'll end up feeling defeated before they even start.

When a school assignment is racist

Whether it's a Thanksgiving craft where children make war bonnets, or curriculum that whitewashes slavery, racism in school work is common. It can be intimidating for children to speak up to their teachers about what they notice, but we can offer coaching and support.

One parent of a kindergartner helped her child respond creatively to a racist assignment. In 2016, 5-year-old Nyemah Greenhouse came home with a school assignment that asked her to "dress up like an Indian." Her mother Tremeka wanted her to skip the assignment. But Nyemah was afraid she would get in trouble.

Tremeka had been following the story of the Dakota Access Pipeline protestors, and she asked Nyemah what she thought of dressing up like a DAPL protestor. Nyemah liked the idea.

Her older sister created a vest for Nyemah that included the statement "water is life", as well as #NODAPL hashtag on it. Tremeka showed Nyemah pictures of the protest and told her why Native Americans were standing up against the pipeline.

In other situations, it may make more sense to request a parent teacher conference.

This kind of speaking up can be anxiety provoking. You can prepare yourself by practicing the main points you'd like to make and using a mindfulness practice to calm yourself.

It can also help to imagine the positive ways a teacher may respond to your concerns. Sometimes a teacher is already ill-at-ease with curriculum materials or longstanding school traditions. Your speaking up may equip the teacher to raise concerns within the school.

For ideas on how to address racism in school Thanksgiving celebrations, see the resources section at the end of the book.

Practice: Take antiracist action as a family

As parents, we're so busy that there's a lot of things we mean to do but never get around to. So right now (yes right now), I want you to pull out your calendar. Mark a date in the near future where your family will plan an action you can take together to challenge racism.

It's helpful to do some background research so that you can offer your kids some options. Is there a vote coming up on a local, state, or national issue that will impact people of color? Is there a company that is providing a platform for white supremacist groups to spread hate speech? Your family could write letters or make phone calls on one of these issues.

If you're not sure how to identify issues and what you can do about them, search online for your city or state's name followed by the plus symbol (+) and add search terms like "immigrant rights organization" or "Black Lives Matter" chapter or "Showing Up for Racial Justice." A few of the organizations that help me take antiracist action are Color of Change, United We Dream, Movement for Black Lives, and the Lakota People's Law Project.

Start following local social justice organizations on social media so that you can find out about times that your family could join a vigil, protest, or public hearing. Again, if you're not already aware of what work is being done, search for "social justice organization" or "community organizing" plus your community's name online.

Let your kids know that while you want them to help decide what specific action you'll take as a family, you are committed to doing <u>something</u>.

Once a family has taken action together a few times, many children will take the lead in thinking of what you can do next.

Resource alert!

Use the worksheet in my free *Raising Antiracist Kids* bonus pack to help you brainstorm action possibilities for your family. Download the pack at antiracistkids.com.

More examples of family activism

I realize that the word "activism" conjures up a very specific image for some people. Maybe this image doesn't match how you see yourself. I think of activism as taking collective action to change unjust policies (whether those are policies of a government, a business, or an organization.)

Others may disagree, but I believe activism includes everything from taking part in a letter writing campaign to joining a candlelight vigil to picketing a business.

If you don't see yourself chanting in public, I have two questions: First, have you ever tried leading kids in a chant? It's seriously fun, as I learned when I led a children's peace and justice camp! If that still doesn't sound appealing, what else can you try? There are ways to take action that fit every personality type, and that set an example for your children of what it means to be actively antiracist.

As Ibram Kendi demonstrates in *How to Be an Antiracist*, there are many racist policies that need to be changed. It's not hard to understand the racist implications of U.S. immigration policy, or school funding that depends on property tax revenue (and therefore benefits whiter, wealthier school districts.) But other issues, including many environmental ones, have racist implications as well.

As Kendi points out, there are nearly 4,000 U.S. communities—most of which are poor and non-white— that have higher lead poisoning rates than Flint, Michigan. Climate change has racial implications as well, hitting communities of color the hardest. These are all examples of where our antiracist activism is needed.

We can encourage our children to embrace activism by asking for their ideas of what we should do.

In the summer of 2018, Shannon Cofrin Gaggero told her two kids, ages 3 and 6, about how children were being taken from their parents at the U.S./Mexico border. She asked her kids what their family could do to help. Her 6-year-old asked about having a lemonade stand.

Gaggero asked her friends on Facebook if anyone would like to participate in a lemonade stand supporting the organization RAICES. They had a virtual stand as well as in-person one led by her children and other kids from their neighborhood. The children made signs that said "kids belong with their families" to hang at the stand. Altogether, the family raised over $13,000.

Gaggero's family got a lot of media attention for the lemonade stand. She emphasizes that her child's idea was the result of years of work with her kids on racial justice issues.

Things to remember

- The early elementary years may be an important developmental window in which cross-racial friendships have the greatest impact.

- Kids need to know that race is not biologically real, but that it is a real concept socially.

- As parents, we can make sure our children learn complex versions of history that they may not be taught in school.

- Speaking up about racist remarks made by family or friends takes courage but is essential modeling for our children.

- Kids need to know that "racist" is a descriptive term of particular ideas, actions, and policies that harm people of color, not a slur that implies someone is beyond the ability to change.

- Metaphors like the moving walkway help kids understand why we must take action to undo systemic racism.

Part V

Antiracist parenting in the middle school years

Some white parents committed to racial justice notice something troubling in their children's teenage years: their teens' worlds have become more segregated. This can even be true for white kids who attend racially diverse schools and had friends of color in preschool and elementary school.

What's going on here? There are several factors at work that influence how our children socialize. I can think of two that are especially prominent in the teen years.

First, academic tracking, which has been shown to be racially biased,[34] intensifies in the middle and high school years. Tracking is used by many schools to separate children into groups according to their perceived academic ability (above average, average, below average) and then assign classes to groups with similar academic ability.

As a result, schools that appear to be racially diverse overall often have a segregated "school within a school" atmosphere because of tracking. White students are much more likely to be given spots in gifted and talented programs, and in honors and Advanced Placement classes, while their peers of color are more likely to steered to standard classes.

Second, research has found that in adolescence, Black youth are much more likely than their white peers to be actively exploring their racial identity. "Why do Black youths, in particular, think about themselves in terms of race?" asks Dr. Beverly Daniel Tatum. **"Because that is how the rest of the world thinks of them."**[35]

Tatum says that being on the receiving end of racism in a direct, personal way often sparks Black teens' exploration of their racial identity. As they investigate who they are racially, they may gravitate towards their Black peers more than they have in the past.

White peers who don't understand the impact racism has on Black teens' lives, or who commit microaggressions against them, intensify this process of separation.

Believing friends of color who've experienced racism

White middle schoolers might notice a growing distance between them and friends of color. One thing that adults can teach white children is that they should believe their friends of color who say they're experiencing racism.

This might sound obvious, but so often white people react to claims of racism with questions that pick apart the incident. What's needed instead is empathy and support. Learning this habit helps white children become better allies. It can also have the side effect of helping kids maintain cross racial friendships.

Imagine, for example, a Latinx teen named Alejandro. On the first day of school, a teacher tells him she'll have to call him Alex instead of Alejandro, because his name is "too hard to say." If Alejandro shares this story with a white friend, how will he feel if that friend tells him, "she probably didn't mean it that way?" He'll likely feel minimized, misunderstood, and angry.

We can encourage our children to think about impact versus intent with questions like these:

- How do you think Alejandro felt when the teacher said she wouldn't use his name? What did he think the bigger message was behind her words?

- Can you think of a time when someone hurt your feelings without meaning to? Did they own up to their mistake, or did they say it shouldn't matter because they didn't mean to hurt you? How did their explanation affect you?

- Do you think what the teacher said to Alejandro will influence how he feels about that class this year?

- What do you think other kids could say to Alejandro that will help him feel understood and supported?

Many white liberal children are used to talking about issues of sexism and homophobia but are less used to identifying racism. When we hear our children talking about examples of other forms of discrimination besides racism, we can affirm how important it is to believe the person who is experiencing bias. This also gives us an opening to remind our kids that the same principle applies to racism.

Of course, we also need to model believing people of color who talk about their experiences of racism. Too often, our white fragility leads us to volunteer other factors we think might have been at play in a situation of discrimination. Instead, we need to affirm what happened was wrong, even if the perpetrator of racism didn't set out to cause harm.

We can also prepare our kids for the fact that they will sometimes say or do things that are racist. How can we encourage kids to think beyond their intentions to the impact of their words on people of color? One way is to discuss what real apologies that are not defensive sound like.

Parents can also share with our teens that it's normal to feel nervous or put on the spot when someone else tells us we've done something racist. But if we want to grow as people, it's important to find ways to receive feedback without being defensive. We can ask our children to think about how nerve-wracking it probably is for a friend of color to speak up to them about racism.

To prepare our kids for times they may feel put on the spot, we can practice phrases like, "I can tell this is really important to you, and I bet it wasn't easy for you to tell me. Thanks. Can I take some time to think about what you said?"

How can we keep white kids from feeling superior?

At first glance, it might seem silly to ask this question. Surely your 7th grader doesn't think that she's better, smarter, or more successful because she's white, does she? But if we look at the racially coded messages our children receive from society, and that white kids send to each other, we have plenty of reason to wrestle with this question.

In her enlightening and troubling ethnographic

study *White Kids: Growing Up with Privilege in a Racially Divided America*, Dr. Margaret Hagerman shares many stories of wealthy white children receiving and sending racist messages.

One day, 12-year-old Edward asked Hagerman if they could stop at a McDonald's on the way home from basketball practice. Edward pointed out that the McDonald's she chose wasn't the one that his parents usually took him too.

After observing a group of Black teens talking and joking as they crossed the parking lot, Edward asked Hagerman "this neighborhood really isn't all that good, is it?" When she asked him why he said that, he replied "it just seems like there are a lot of poor people around here. We don't usually stop here. My mom says it's dangerous." Hagerman reports that just a few weeks earlier when she asked him an explicit question about race, Edward told her "we are all the same. Race doesn't really matter anymore."[36]

Antiracism experts often talk about how racism and its many messages of white supremacy are similar to smog. We all breath in the racist smog. We can't keep it from entering our lungs.

So, I don't want to imply there is some foolproof system for keeping white kids from internalizing messages of false racial superiority. Some of those messages will still get through, despite our best efforts. But we can find ways to ways to pierce that false sense of superiority, so that our kids can see the lies that white supremacy is telling them.

As a parent, I want my children to be comfortable in their own skin and not be ashamed to be white. I also want them to root their confidence in authentic sources, not in their whiteness.

Here are just a few ideas about how to deflate the sense of white superiority society encourages children to have:

- Teach kids about the existence of racism in the past and present, including white people's roles in perpetuating racism. Often, we talk about racism as if it happened by accident, rather than being a system that is created and maintained by white people to give white people unfair advantages. As we have these conversations, we also need to show kids that as white people, we have the choice to be antiracist rather than upholding racism.

- Show kids that we're open to their race-related observations by asking questions that start a dialogue, instead of giving a lecture. Middle school age children can give us valuable insights about the realities of racism, especially when they know we genuinely want to hear what they think. For example, if your child remarks that most of the kids who get suspended at her school are Black, you could ask:
    - Why do you think that might be?
    - Does that bother you?
    - Have you ever heard adults notice that too? What did they say about it?
    - If you asked some of the Black students at your school about why this is happening, what do you think they'd say?

- Think carefully about racially coded messages adults may be sending children when we use phrases like "good neighborhoods," "good schools," and "hardworking people."

Looking at our use of coded racist language

One way that parents contribute to white kids' sense of racial superiority is our use of coded racist language. Some of this language is so commonplace that we might not even realize what is racist about it. When we jokingly using terms like "thug" or "ghetto," we send racist messages about Black people being dangerous and their neighborhoods being impoverished and unsafe.

One day when I logged onto Facebook, I saw a picture of two white teens I have a close relationship with. They were gathered with their friends, and all of the teens were using fake "gang signs." All of them attended schools where there are few Black students. They've also had little in-depth contact in their lives with Black people of any age.

I reached out to them, explaining to them that the photo was hurtful and offensive to Black teens, even though I know they didn't intend it to be. I reminded them of the different ways that white and Black teens are perceived, and that their photo played into those stereotypes. I shared that a similar photo had been getting attention and causing a lot of hurt among Black students at a college in my city.

My young friends expressed appreciation that I'd gotten in touch about the photo. Even though I felt anxiety about speaking to them, it reminded me how important it is to interrupt this kind of behavior instead of ignoring it.

Even white people who wouldn't use words like thug or ghetto frequently talk about "good schools" and "bad neighborhoods" (sometimes substituting words like "sketchy" and "shady.") I've used this language myself many times in the past.

White parents often use this language when we're describing why we chose particular neighborhoods or schools for our families. We imply that we're using objective criteria that parents of any race would agree with as we make these choices.

Particularly when it comes to choosing schools though, research suggests that white parents rely more on word of mouth recommendations from fellow white parents. The research finds we also tend to judge schools by the racial makeup of the neighborhood they're located in, rather than examining criteria like average test scores.

Sociologist Heather Beth Johnson found that "parents tied a school's reputation directly to the race and class composition of its students."[37] This is one reason I'm doing my best to stop using the language of good and bad neighborhoods and schools.

For one, my judgments about which schools are "better" or "worse" are rooted in racist ideas. Second, I've considered how hurtful it would be for any child to hear their neighborhood or school labelled as "bad." Finally, using coded language teaches my children that their white privilege and class privilege makes them better people than kids of color and poor children.

White middle schoolers' ideas about race and biology

Children of all ages are continually making observations about race. The older they get, the more likely they are to notice differences in power and privilege. Whether they talk to adults about their observations or not, they're trying to make sense of what they see.

While researching *White Kids*, Hagerman overheard a lot of discussion about race between the white middle schoolers she studied. While talking about basketball players one afternoon, a 12-year-old insisted to his friend that Black basketball players must have an extra muscle in their legs. He was sure this must be the case, because he saw how many star basketball players are Black. A different child asked Hagerman if "Asian kids are actually smarter than white kids?"[38]

These middle schoolers noticed patterns. **Without proper adult guidance, they assumed that biology, not systemic inequality, was the cause of the patterns they observe.**

Many of these conversations about race are happening when parents aren't around. How can we know what's being said out of earshot? There's no denying that it can be hard to get tweens and young teens to open up to us.

We can start by asking ourselves whether we're still sending any messages to kids that they should be colorblind. I noticed in *White Kids* that many of the children whose observations were the most blatantly racist lived in families that either encouraged them to be colorblind or who had hostile attitudes toward Black and Latinx people. When kids have gotten the message that it's not okay to talk about race, they're certainly not going to ask us puzzling questions.

But even in families that strive to be antiracist and talk openly about race, kids may be hesitant to tell us what they think.

I don't advocate snooping on our kids or violating their privacy. But we can listen when we're driving them and their friends to soccer practice, or when they're hanging out in the kitchen together. What kind of anecdotes kids tell each other can give us clues to the conversations we need to have.

That still leaves the sticky situation of how to answer questions kids do come right out and ask us, like "why do all the Latino kids live in that bad neighborhood?" First, we need to validate the question. A parent could say something like "I see that you're noticing that race makes a difference in how people live, and what advantages they do or don't have. I'm glad you asked me."

Just as we do with younger children, we can then ask them first whether they have any ideas. This gives us a chance to see what conclusions our kids are already starting to make, so that we'll know if there are biases or incorrect assumptions that need to be gently corrected. With this particular question, it's also important to ask what our child thinks makes a neighborhood "bad."

Finally, with a question about racism that doesn't have one simple answer, we could say something like, "I bet this is a question other people have wondered about. It's probably even something that professors have done research about. What would you think about us looking together to see if we can find some of that research?"

Not only does this help guide our children toward the systemic injustices at play in this situation (rather than blaming individual people), it also helps parents become more articulate about the problem ourselves.

Practice: Help kids recognize their own white privilege

In 1989, Dr. Peggy McIntosh wrote an article entitled "White Privilege: Unpacking the Invisible Knapsack," which has been used to help countless white people understand concrete examples of how white privilege works. In the article, she shares 50 unfair advantages that she regularly experiences because of being white. Middle school age children can relate to many of the examples, with an adult's help.

Talking through the article as a family is one way to help your child identify what unearned benefits they receive because of their whiteness. It will also help you think about how white privilege works in your life, and ways that you can disrupt that privilege in your daily life. (The article can be found at racialequitytools.org/resourcefiles/mcintosh.pdf)

Here are a few examples of white privilege that teens should be able to identify with. Some are directly from McIntosh, others are adapted from her work, and some are from me.

- When I'm told about our nation's history, I'm shown that people of my color made it what it is.
- If I want to, I can arrange to be around people of my race most of the time.

- When I see police officers, I don't have to think about how I walk or talk in order to keep myself safe.

- If I raise my hand in class, I can be pretty sure the teacher will call on me eventually.

- Most of the time, my teachers will be of my same race.

- When I go shopping, I can be pretty sure I won't be followed around the store or harassed.

- If I wear the hood of my sweatshirt up at school, I can be pretty sure I won't get in serious trouble for it.

- I am never asked to speak for all the people of my racial group.

Disrupting the phrase "that's so racist"

One day in eighth grade art class, I turned to a white friend and asked him to pass me a piece of black construction paper. "That's so racist!" he said with a smile. At the time, I thought his joke was kind of weird.

Fast forward to today, when joking about things being racist that are not actually racist is incredibly widespread among teens. In fact, in one suburban middle school profiled in *White Kids*, this became such a problem that school administrators added "racist" to a list of words children weren't allowed to use. Other words on the list included "fag" and "gay."[39]

Kids live in a society that teaches them confusing and conflicting messages about race. They're told many of the following things:

- Being racist is very, very bad.

- We're all the same inside.

- Talking about race is rude and offensive.

- Racism is the fault of a minority of individual, backwards thinking people.

So, even though it's disturbing that kids turn "you're so racist" into a joke, it's not surprising.

Kids joke about things that are clearly a big deal to adults, but that are also hard to understand. As parents, we must disrupt the use of "that's so racist" as a joke or insult.

Blogger Carrie Hutchinson suggests starting with something like "When I hear the way you use the word 'racist,' it makes me worried that you may not understand what the word means. Can we talk about it?"[40] This opening gives us a chance to talk about what the word racism does mean. See examples on page 70 you can use to describe racism to your child.

For adolescents, you could also unpack Ibram Kendi's definition of racism, that it is "a powerful collection of racist policies that lead to racial inequity and are substantiated by racist ideas."

The most important thing to communicate in this conversation is that racism causes real harm to people of color. Noticing race is not racist, and we can't undo racism if we don't talk about race. When we jokingly label things racist that have nothing to do with racism, we send people of color a signal that we don't think racism matters.

When kids feel guilty about being white

Earlier, I shared research that shows Black teens are more likely than their white peers to explore their racial identity. But white youth and young adults who take time to learn about the realities of racism go through their own process of racial development, figuring out what it means to be white. I'll share more about the stages of white racial development in section VI.

Teens (and in some cases, older elementary children) who are wrestling with whiteness will likely go through stages of guilt, shame, and resentment. You may be feeling some of these things yourself as you go deeper into the journey of antiracism. Our children need our help in working through their feelings of guilt, which are a typical part of racial development.

We want to empathize with our kids, and we also need to help them move beyond guilt so that they can find ways to take action against racism. Otherwise, the "act" of feeling guilty for being white can feel like a sufficient substitute for real action.

While we shouldn't exaggerate to our children how many white people choose to engage in antiracism, we need to show them that being antiracist can be part of their white identity. This doesn't mean teaching our kids simplistic thinking, such as telling them they should try to be "one of the good white people." It means supporting people of color as they fight racism and taking action in the places where we have influence.

Jennifer Harvey points out that we can also explore the sense of responsibility being white gives us when it comes to engaging in antiracism work. When talking with her child about the fact that one of her ancestors owned slaves, Harvey told her child that this family history is one of the reasons that she's committed to racial justice.

She stressed to her child that "we can always make different choices than our ancestors did...It's our job to actively make different choices and work for justice and fairness today, especially if we're white."[41]

Pause and Reflect

Use the worksheet in my free *Raising Antiracist Kids* bonus pack to think about how you can help your children deal with feelings of guilt. Download the pack at antiracistkids.com.

What does it mean to be antiracist?

In part V, we introduced a definition of racism that Jennifer Harvey has used with her elementary age children. It points to systemic racism in a way that elementary kids can still grasp.

By the middle school years, we can go even deeper in our understandings of the ways that racism is much more than personal racial prejudice. One way to do this is to explore what it means to be antiracist with our children.

Ibram Kendi describes racist ideas as "any idea that suggests one racial group is inferior or superior to another racial group in any way." In contrast, antiracist ideas are ideas that suggest "the racial groups are equals in all their apparent differences—that there is nothing right or wrong with any racial group. Antiracist ideas argue that racist policies are the cause of racial inequities."[42]

Let's say a white 12-year-old notices that while the majority of the students in her school are either Black or Latinx, most of the kids in her honors Algebra class are white. We could tell this child about how Kendi describes the difference between racist and antiracist ideas. Then we could ask, "what have you heard from other people about why your Algebra class looks different than the overall school? What are your ideas?"

As she identifies these ideas, we can ask about each one: "Do you think that is a racist idea about why this situation is happening, or an antiracist idea?"

Antiracist explanations for the disparity might include the following:

- Internalized racial bias on the part of teachers about which students are smart, hard-working, or have an aptitude for math. These biases can keep Black and Latinx students from getting the teacher recommendation they need to enroll in an honors class.

- The financial resources for tutoring that white parents are more likely to have in order to get their children placed in the Algebra class, so that they are more likely to pass an entrance test.

- The knowledge about how to "work the system" in a child's favor that is passed through networks of white parents, especially those who are middle class or above. For example, if a standardized test is required to get into the class, some parents may be able to pay privately to have their child re-tested after failing the exam.

In contrast, racist explanations for why a child's honors class is segregated might include thinking that Black and Latinx parents don't care as much about their kids' education or that these children are more likely to come from "broken homes."

Having this kind of conversation with your child might make you nervous. What if your child expresses a racist idea to explain the racial makeup of her honors class? There's a good chance that could happen, if not in this particular conversation, perhaps in another one. When that happens, we need to ask more questions that can help our kids see where their thinking slipped into racism.

The other thing that gives me courage to have these conversations is knowing that we're going to have hundreds more talks about race. Some of these talks may last 90 seconds, while others go on for 20 minutes. If I realize I've gotten something wrong, or there's more I want to add, I can always ask my kids, "Can we pick up that conversation we had the other day?"

We can also remind our kids of something else that is key to Kendi's work: the idea that no one is forever racist or antiracist. These labels, he says, "are not permanent tattoos," because they are always contingent on what ideas we're expressing or what work we are doing in that particular moment. He writes:

No one becomes a racist or antiracist. We can only strive to be one or the other...Like fighting an addiction, being an antiracist requires persistent self-awareness, constant self-criticism, and regular self-examination."[43]

Addressing racist stereotypes that come from tracking

A few school districts across the country are starting to question academic tracking, recognizing the ways it reinforces racial inequality. Still, for the majority of children in public schools, tracking is a reality.

There are two types of stereotypes that tracking encourages in white kids. The first are racist ideas about Black, Latinx, and Native students caring less about school or being less intelligent. The second are racist ideas about Asian students related to the model minority myth.

When we hear our kids reflect the frequently repeated lie that Black and Latinx parents care less about their children's education, we need to disrupt that. An expansive survey by *Education Post*, for example, found that higher percentages of Black and Latinx parents than white parents thought going to college was very important for their own child, as well as for children in general.[44]

If a child observes that more white parents attend school functions than Latinx parents, we can ask thoughtful questions about why that might be. First, is that observation correct, or does it just seem that way to our child?

Second, what times are events being scheduled, and does the timing make it challenging for parents working hourly jobs to attend? Are younger siblings welcome at these events, and if not, how does that affect who can take part? Is there an interpreter available for

104

parents whose first language isn't English?

We also need to think about stereotypes white kids are forming about Asian Americans as the "model minority." When it comes to the model minority myth, kids might not be able to see at first what's wrong with it. If we're saying something positive about someone, then what's the problem?

Educator Sarah-SoonLing Blackburn has shared her own experience about the harm this stereotype causes. In 11th grade, her pre-calculus teacher pulled her into the hallway to tell her he was disappointed in her test grade. "You can do better than this," he told her. "I'm surprised by grades like this from someone like you."

Blackburn's teacher assumed that because she was Asian, she had a natural aptitude for math and should be earning straight A's. While other students were offered extra help with concepts they didn't understand, she was left to flounder.[45]

Additionally, the model minority myth erases differences between Asian Americans, a group that includes many different countries and cultures. There are also large differences in social class among Asian immigrants, partly based on which countries people emigrated from.

Finally, the model minority myth erases racism that Asian Americans face by holding them up as a group to be emulated.

The need for kids of color to have their own spaces

Colorblind culture talks about segregation (in

which people are separated by race in order to maintain a racial hierarchy with white people at the top) and separation (in which people of color carve out their own protective spaces) as the same thing. It's likely our kids will hear people say things like the now famous title of Beverly Daniel Tatum's book: why *are* all the Black kids sitting together in the cafeteria? They may ask us, "isn't that racist?"

By middle school, kids may also be hearing anti-affirmative action messages, claiming that programs specifically designed for Black and Latinx students are unfair or even "reverse racism." As parents, we can resist these racist messages ourselves. We also need to ask our kids questions that help them think about why spaces and programs specifically for people of color are needed.

For a child who notices the Black table in the cafeteria, we could initiate a conversation with questions like the following:

- "You're paying attention to race and asking questions about why that matters. I'm glad you're doing that. Have you ever wondered what the cafeteria might look like to the Black students?"

- "At your school, when Black kids and white kids do hang out together, do you think it's usually white kids who approach Black kids to talk, or is it mostly the other way around? Do you think it matters who takes the first step?"

- "Can you think of some conversations that might be easier for Black students to have with other Black kids than with white kids?"

As we consider formal programs designed to help students of color overcome barriers to academic success, we can help our white kids unpack the reasons why these programs are needed.

We can approach these conversations by talking about the unfair advantages white families like ours have. These advantages include implicit bias and structural racism that works in our kids' favor, frequent social connections with school leadership, and much more.

Now that our middle schoolers are old enough to have learned some American history, we could do a family research project or pop quiz (keeping in mind that it shouldn't feel too much like school.) We can explore questions like:

- How many centuries have Native Americans lived in what is now called the United States? When did white settlers began to arrive? When did the era of forced Indian boarding schools end?

- When were Africans first brought to the country as slaves? How many centuries did slavery last? How many years after that was segregation legal? And how many years have passed since segregation ended? There are graphics available online that help illustrate how white supremacy was the law of the land for most of U.S. history.[46]

- Does this history of discrimination seem like it was a long time ago, or pretty recent? Do you think some of your Black or Native American classmates might have grandparents who lived under Jim Crow segregation or the boarding school era?

Alternately, we can ask our kids questions about the differences they notice in how Black, Latinx, Native American, Asian, and white students experience school.

107

Who tends to get placed in which classes? Do some teachers tend to bend certain rules for white students but not students of color (perhaps without realizing they're doing it?)

Once they've identified a couple of differences, we can wonder with our kids how the day to day experiences of students of color might impact their attitudes about school. How could having a space with other students of color help them deal with the frequent discrimination they experience?

Supporting kids as they take action at school

By the time they enter the middle school years, kids who've been raised in an antiracist manner are often primed to take action. The ways they want to challenge racism may go beyond speaking up when they hear someone express prejudice.

In *White Kids*, 12-year-old Danny complained about teachers who only wanted them to learn from textbooks rather than talking about problems "in the real world." He was so eager for teachers to "give us something to do, like this is something *you* can do to stop it, let's go out into the world and help stop it!"[47]

Once children become attuned to racism, they will likely start noticing it in places that we have missed (or taken it for granted). For example, several of the children interviewed for *White Kids* noted that there is a "no hoods up" rule at their school about sweatshirts. Yet, some of the children realized, white children are frequently allowed to break this rule while Black children are not.[48]

While we shouldn't force our children to take action, as caregivers we can create conditions that support them in acting when they are ready. **We need to affirm that the examples they bring to us are racism, and that our children are right to be upset by them.** We can ask our kids what they wish would be different.

With the hoodie example, we could ask if they feel that the no hoods up rule should be abolished. Would they like to see a big group of students come together to protest it? Or do they think the rule is okay, but it should be fairly enforced?"

Taking time for this imagining is more than just wish fulfillment. It reminds our kids that we don't have to accept racism as inevitable.

We can help our kids strategize about what first and second steps could be. Do they have relationships with any students of color who've expressed frustration about the no hoods up rule? Can they identify other white kids who are bothered by this? Is there a teacher who would support them in making a plan? What kind of support would your child like from you?

Another longer-term way to help kids take antiracist action is suggested by Jennifer Harvey in *Raising White Kids*. Harvey wonders about the potential of antiracist clubs in schools, similar to the Gay Straight Alliances that are present in so many schools today.[49] For kids who are especially attuned to racial injustice, we can ask them what they think a club could accomplish at their school. We can offer to help them approach a teacher who might make a good sponsor for such a group.

Supporting kids who speak up (even when they're not polite)

As I shared in the introduction, I had a great aunt who used almost every Thanksgiving dinner as an opportunity to say something racist about Black people. For years, the adults tended to ignore her and try to change the subject. But one year, my cousin (her grandson) had apparently had enough. He was in college by then, and I suspect he'd developed more friendships with Black classmates.

When my great aunt started up her usual talk, he just looked at her and said, "Aw Gran, shut up." His tone wasn't mean, but it was also clear that he meant it. And shut up she did. I don't remember her ever saying anything openly racist again at Thanksgiving.

Was my cousin polite? No. But he had the courage to do what none of our parents' generation had done by letting her know that he didn't want to hear her racist comments.

I share this example because the middle school years are tough in general, filled with lots of emotion. Kids who've been raised with antiracist ideas may express their beliefs passionately, angrily, and clumsily. We can coach them on how to say what they're feeling without demeaning the person they're addressing. **But we also need to honor their courage so that we don't accidentally send the message that everyone would be happier if they kept quiet.**

We can teach our kids that some situations require a call-out to the person who's using hateful speech. Public call-outs are also appropriate in situations where someone has repeatedly refused to acknowledge the harm that they're causing others. Yet other situations, such as someone making a statement out of ignorance, may be better suited to calling someone in.

Loretta J. Ross has written an excellent article for *Teaching Tolerance* on how teachers can create "call-in culture" in the classroom. She shares that "calling-in is speaking up without tearing down."

A call-in may be public or private, she writes, but "its key feature is that it's done with love." Instead of shaming someone who's made a mistake, call-ins take the time to ask questions that help the listener understand why someone used the harmful words they did.

One questions that Ross suggests for teachers that middle schoolers could also use in everyday situations is, "Do you think you would say that if someone from that group was with us right now?"[50]

Practice: Antiracist media literacy

As a sarcastic middle schooler, I loved pointing out the things I thought were dumb about advertisements. Once I realized that I was being emotionally manipulated so that I would buy things, I couldn't stop seeing that pattern.

My middle school self was practicing a simplistic form of media literacy.

Parents can help children practice a more nuanced version of media literacy that develops their radar for racist messaging in advertising, books, television shows, movies, YouTube videos, and more.

As we recognize these racist messages, we need to talk about what is specifically is wrong with them, and what antiracist truth could correct the racist lie we're witnessing. Use the examples on the following pages to practice at least one form of media literacy with your children.

Talking about advertising's racist messages about beauty

Our kids are exposed to a huge amount of advertising, much of it related to beauty, fashion, and bodies. This gives us countless opportunities to look at messages about beauty, and how these messages are racialized.

In a bookstore or drugstore that has a magazine display, look at the covers of the women's magazines. Flip through them to find advertisements for makeup and clothing. How many of the magazines have photos of white women, and how many of them have women of color?

Of the photos of women of color, how many of them are women who have darker shades of skin, or do the Black and Latinx models and celebrities mostly have light or medium shades of skin? What physical attributes show up on covers and in ads repeatedly?

If you have a child who's interested in makeup, head next to the makeup aisles. How many different shades of foundation are available, especially from the largest brands?

Discussing news coverage

Even if it doesn't seem like your kid is paying much attention to the news, they are listening to snippets of TV or radio coverage, hearing mentions of hot-button stories from friends, and likely talking about some current events in the classroom.

My husband and I found out the hard way that we should be initiating more conversations about the news with my stepson. He was in high school when Ferguson police officer Darren Wilson shot and killed Michael Brown, an unarmed Black teenager. After protests exploded in Ferguson, my stepson mentioned that they had a debate in one of his classes about events there.

When we asked him what he thought about all of it, he said something along the lines of "he shouldn't have been shot, and I see why people are upset. But they aren't helping anything by rioting in their own neighborhoods." My husband and I locked eyes as if we'd just heard a record scratch.

After taking a deep breath, my husband started a conversation that helped my stepson understand the roots of the Ferguson protests. A few months later I took him to hear Rev. Osagyefo Uhuru Sekou, a clergy leader from the protests, talk about his experiences.

Seeing how much our son's perspective shifted after these conversations made me wonder about what opportunities we had already missed.

As you look at news coverage with your children, ask them: who do you think is telling this story? How might their race influence the way they are telling it? You might even compare what facts about a story are told in differing publications (including news outlets led by people of color such as *Indian Country Today*, *Essence*, *Univision*, *Al Jazeera America,* and *AsAmNews*.)

Identifying white saviorism in movies

We can also teach middle schoolers to watch out for themes of white saviorism. White savior movies and stories show people of color who are victimized by racism, and who also need white people with more power than them to free them from the situation.

White savior movies that are based on true stories exaggerate the roles that white allies played in ending racism. At the same time, they diminish the skills, strategies, and self-determination that people of color used to achieve freedom. They show white people as heroes when they are doing what any decent human should do, while implying that Black people standing up for themselves is to simply be expected, not admired.

Famous movies that include white savior themes are *Hidden Figures*, *The Help*, and *To Kill a Mockingbird*, to name just a few.

One way to practice media literacy is to watch previews of movies that are about racial injustice. Ask your child: who seems to have prominent roles in the preview? Are people of color shown as needing help from white people who are more powerful than them? Based on the preview, who do you think is telling this story? (In other words, what do you think the race of the director, producer, or screenwriter is?)

If you want to have some fun with this process, watch the clip "White Savior: The Movie Trailer" from *Late Night with Seth Meyers*.[51]

Avoiding white saviorism while volunteering

Middle schoolers are figuring out their place in the world and how they can challenge the problems that trouble them so deeply. That's a very good thing. **But for** white children, especially white kids who also hold class privilege, it's easy for passion to turn towards white saviorism.

As parents, we can think about what kind of settings we volunteer in, and what messages we give our children about why we volunteer. We can look for organizations that fully uphold the dignity of their clients and partner with them, rather than looking down on people.

When we're volunteering in a social service setting, we can replace language about "the needy" or "the less fortunate" with language that acknowledges the systemic injustice that requires people to seek help in the first place.

On the way to volunteering at the food pantry, we can remind our kids that many of the people who are there to pick up food are working, but their wages are low. This is also a chance to remind young teens that the work low-wage workers do is incredibly important to our communities. But it's work that is typically looked down on by people who hold class privilege, especially if the workers are Black or Brown.

One powerful way to reinforce this message about systemic injustice is to pair our community service with social justice action. After volunteering at the food pantry, we could write our members of Congress about increasing the minimum wage.

In tutoring or mentoring situations, we also need to watch for signs that a teen thinks they're a child's "best hope" of success in life. When we catch a teen (or ourselves) thinking this way, we can remind them that we're just a brief part of this child's life. There are surely parents, grandparents, aunts, uncles, and community members who are playing a much larger role than us in encouraging this child to dream about and work toward their future.

As we consider activist organization working for social change, we can ask questions about how many people of color are in their leadership.

When engaging in activism, such as participating in a vigil against police brutality, adults can talk about how we're there to show our support for black community members who are taking action. We can remind our kids (and ourselves) that amplifying their message when we're in white spaces could be even more important than showing up at the protest itself.

Pause and Reflect

Use the worksheet in my free *Raising Antiracist Kids* bonus pack to reflect on the experiences you and your children have had with white saviorism. Download the pack at antiracistkids.com.

Things to remember

- White kids' peers of color are becoming more aware of how racism impacts them. We can help our teens be good friends by teaching them not to be defensive when racism is called out.

- Middle school age children often get basic factual information about race wrong. We must directly address the stereotypes they are absorbing.

- We can use specific strategies to keep white teens from feeling neither superior because of their race, nor feeling that being white can only equal being racist.

- Middle schoolers are old enough to understand the systemic aspects of racism.

- Educational tracking intensifies in middle school. It's important for parents to address and interrupt the racist stereotypes kids may be absorbing from tracking.

- We can practice antiracist media literacy with our kids as we watch movie trailers and look at ads and magazines.

- It's important to identify white saviorism, so that we can avoid it when we take action.

Part VI

Challenging ourselves and sustaining our journeys

Parenting my kids using an antiracist framework requires me to repeatedly go deeper in challenging racism, both within myself and in the world. I can't do antiracism work with my children unless I'm doing my own work too.

I believe that antiracism work is deeply emotional work. It is spiritual work. It's work that's best done in community. Standing up to racism requires us to resist the culture of white silence. This culture invites us to embrace our white privilege while ignoring the countless ways racism harms people of color. It's not easy to engage in that continual resistance. It's crucial that we reach out to others, and that we develop spiritual, mental, and emotional practices that can sustain our growth.

In this section, I offer ideas for engaging in antiracism work beyond our conversations with our children. I also share resources to sustain us as we engage in this challenging work long-term.

Learning the stages of racial development

In section V, we talked briefly about teen's racial identity development. Now, let's learn more about the six stages of white racial identity development so that we can understand both our children and ourselves.

119

Racial identity development can happen at any age, from childhood through adulthood. It's also possible, and common, for people to move forward in their racial identity development, only to move back a stage when change becomes overwhelming.

Over the past year-and-a-half, as I have been pushing myself to go deeper in my antiracism work, I've noticed myself moving back and forth between the racial identity stages identified by psychologist Janet Helms.

I'll briefly address the stages below, but I encourage you to read a more in-depth description in either *Why Are All the Black Kids Sitting Together in the Cafeteria* by Beverly Daniel Tatum or *Raising White Kids* by Jennifer Harvey.

The first stage of white racial identity development that Helms identifies is *contact*. In the contact stage, most white people are unaware that they are being continually socialized into whiteness and a sense of white superiority.

White parents in this stage don't realize that the choices available to us in terms of housing, schools, and children's products are strongly shaped by racism and white supremacy.[52]

The second stage is *disintegration*. Disintegration is marked by an awareness that not everyone is treated equally. For example, a white woman who personally witnesses a racist incident involving her child's Black classmate might move into disintegration because of what she saw. Becoming close friends with a person of color can also force a white person to acknowledge that racism exists.

Often, the disintegration stage is accompanied by a strong desire to withdraw from the places and situations that are making the person aware of racism. Other white people in this stage may react differently, taking it upon themselves to zealously point out every instance of other people's racism to their peers.[53]

The third stage is ***reintegration***. Because noticing racism is painful, white people feel a strong desire to relieve themselves from that pain. In the reintegration stage, their feelings of guilt or shame turn to anger or fear directed at people of color.

White people in the reintegration stage may wish that people of color would stop "making such a big deal" out of racism. Or they may try hard to prove that they are one of the "good white people," not like the others who have caused racism.[54]

White parents experiencing reintegration might boast of sending their kids to multicultural schools. Another parent experiencing disintegration might tell others that it's not racism that causes segregation in the local schools. Instead, he blames parents of color who aren't involved in their children's schools.

The fourth stage is ***pseudo-independence***. White people who enter this stage move beyond blaming people of color. They are willing to take on racism that exists within themselves. Beverly Daniel Tatum points out that some people would describe a person in this stage as the "guilty white liberal" who has an intellectual understanding of racism but isn't sure what to do with what they've learned.[55]

This stage can be accompanied by white people distancing themselves from other whites and mostly associating with people of color. For example, white parents experiencing pseudo-independence can be over-eager to talk with moms of color about racism they observe.

White antiracist parents who don't have other white allies to talk to often put unfair burdens on people of color. Tatum points out that a white person telling a story about a racist incident they need to process "to a person of color may reopen that person's wounds. Listening to those stories and problem-solving about them is a job that white people can do for each other."[56]

The fifth stage is *immersion/emersion*. In this stage, white people recognize that they cannot escape their whiteness, but they can live out their whiteness in an antiracist way. Jennifer Harvey says that in this stage "we move from experiencing being white in a reductive sense—as in I-am-innately-only-bad-and-always-racist."[57]

White parents in this stage see how they are deeply impacted by racism, yet they're also willing to take risks and change their past patterns to challenge racism. They find ways to connect with other white people engaged in antiracism work, including those who can support them as they continue their journey.[58]

The sixth and final stage is *autonomy*. White people in this stage are committed to continually learning more about racism and how it shapes their reality. They are more likely to be willing to challenge racism without waiting for a person of color to speak up first. Yet, as Harvey points out, they also understand they must be accountable to people of color as they engage in antiracism.[59]

Understanding these stages, and the fact that we can move backwards a stage or two as we try to unlearn racism, has been helpful to me. When I found myself irritated by an Asian friend's complaints about white people tone policing her on Facebook, I thought, "maybe she's just being too sensitive." After some reflection, I realized that I'd moved backwards in my racial

122

development into the reintegration stage.

Being familiar with these stages reminds me that my goal is do the work that helps me arrive at the autonomy stage, and that helps me stay there. Understanding racial identity development also makes me aware of how my children may react when confronted with the realities of racism.

Sometimes we wonder if it would have been better to put off a particular conversation about racism until our child is older. For example, if they rejoice that they don't face racism because they're white, did we do more harm than good by pointing out racism to them?

If we continue our ongoing work of helping our kids understand racism, if we commit to having conversation after conversation, we can be fairly sure that our children will eventually move forward in their racial identity development.

Addressing guilt, shame, and perfectionism

In section III, I cautioned against using shame or guilt as we help a child understand why something they did was racist. Now, I encourage you to move past any shame or guilt you feel as you recall racist things you did in the past.

We receive racist messages day in and day out. There's no way to shield ourselves from the effects of these messages 100 percent of the time. Having racist thoughts or having done racist things doesn't make us fundamentally flawed people.

These realizations do bring us the opportunity for

change. When we say yes to that opportunity to change, we find that there are always more ways we can dismantle racism within ourselves and challenge racism in our culture.

Antiracism is not a job that we can ever say that we've finished. There are times when it's been very hard for me to stay in this work because I'm so disappointed with myself. Why do I keep making mistakes? What should I do about the conversation I just flubbed with my kid? Will there ever be a time when I felt like all my life choices align to express my antiracist commitment?

When one of my mentors, Jardana Peacock, explained to me that perfectionism is rooted in white supremacy, it was transformational for me. She helped me see that I've been trained as a white person to think it's possible for me to know the answers, to always be right. That same culture tells me that I should always be in control of myself and the situations around me. When it turns out that I don't know the answer, or I cannot control a situation, I feel shame.

Antiracist trainers Tema Okun and Kenneth Jones describe how perfectionism rooted in white supremacy sees "mistakes as being personal." They write that "making a mistake is confused with being a mistake."[60]

Because of white supremacist culture, they write, the person who's made a mistake, "focuses on inadequacies and mistakes rather than learning from them; the person works with a harsh and constant inner critic." [61]

As white parents, we will make mistakes. Even if we've been doing antiracism work for years, we will make mistakes. There's a good chance our white fragility will show up when we make a mistake. That fragility might prompt us to defend ourselves by talking about our

124

intentions. Or we may find ourselves headed in the opposite direction, shaming ourselves for what we've done and withdrawing from others because we feel unworthy.

Neither approach is healthy. Neither approach helps us engage in the work of antiracism.

If we're not willing to find ways to let go of our perfectionism, we will pass it on to our children. We'll become too frustrated with them when our first (or second or third) conversation about racism doesn't have the effect we were hoping for. We may compare them with other kids who seem to "get it" and are even mobilizing others to take action. That frustration and those comparisons become toxic, to us and to our kids.

Mistakes, whether our children's or our own, do not fundamentally define who we are. Internalizing that message takes time and mental and emotional space. Believing that mistakes don't define us also prepares us to receive feedback from others about how racism is showing up in our lives.

As we learn from our mistakes, we show our kids what it means to live with humility and courage at the same time. As we make mistakes and receive feedback, it's important that we have relationships with other white people who are on an antiracist journey.

It's very common for white people to turn to people of color when we want to talk about racism we've witnessed or been accused of. I can think of so many times that I've done this. But doing this requires heavy emotional labor from people of color who are already experiencing trauma from racism.

As we start talking more about race and racism, we can look for other white people who want to raise their children in a similar way. We might find other white antiracist parents at our school or house of worship, or in a more formal group like a Showing Up for Racial Justice chapter. When we're not sure where we can find these people in real life, we can join online communities. See the resources section at the end of the book, I've included information about an interactive reflection circle I lead which helps participants develop relationships with other white parents committed to antiracism.

Examining our choices as parents

As my kids have grown older, I've become more aware of both the benefits of, and the limits to, talking about race with them. White parents who talk openly about race in an antiracist manner are unfortunately still in the minority.

We must break the silence that white people are encouraged to keep, because that silence allows racism to continue unchecked. Our kids can't challenge racism if they can't identify it first. **At the same time, the conversations we have about race are only part of what influences our kids' worldview.** Their day to day life experiences also have a big impact on the motivation they feel (or don't feel) to challenge racism.

Reflecting on what she learned from her in-depth study of 36 affluent white middle schoolers, Margaret Hagerman urges parents to go beyond talking about race (especially if those conversations are only occasional and prompted by tragedies such as police shootings). Beyond conversation, Hagerman writes:

...it is even more important that parents think about the larger social environment that they construct for their child, thinking about what they

126

do in addition to what they say. Choices about homes, schools, vacations, social networks, extracurricular activities, media, language, and so forth play a key role in shaping young people's racial views.[62]

Some of the choices that Hagerman lists are easier to examine than others.

One place that we can start is to question the conventional wisdom among white parents about school choices. Recently, a mom told me about how excited her daughter was to start kindergarten at a school that's widely respected in her community. The student body is a mix of children who live in the mostly Latinx neighborhood near the school, and a smaller number of mostly white children from outside the neighborhood who are admitted through the school system's honors program.

As the time came to officially enroll, other white parents kept telling this mom that it was really important that she request one of two kindergarten teachers who were known as "the best." But when she requested these teachers, her child was assigned another teacher.

Again, parent friends told her that she needed to contact the principal, because that's "what was done." She did, but the principal still kept her child in her original class assignment.

A month after school started, she saw that her child was adjusting well and loved her teacher. Most of her classmates are Latinx, and her daughter has developed an interest in learning Spanish after hearing her teacher speak it with some of the kids.

As the mom spent more time in the new school, she noticed that almost all the white kindergarteners were in one of the two classrooms that other parents told her she "had" to get her child into. "It felt kind of gross to me once I realized what was happening," she said. She saw how segregation was taking place within a school whose overall demographics made it seem diverse.

This mom's story is a typical example of how white middle class parents interact with public schools. Too often, we use our white privilege to benefit our own kids, without asking how our advocacy plays into larger patterns of segregation and bias.

When I think about all the factors on Margaret Hagerman's list of what affects our children's racial development, at times I feel overwhelmed. It took our family a long time transfer our younger son to an integrated school. There are other choices that I need to make over-and-over, like the words I use. There are still other questions that my family hasn't examined at all yet, such as the predominantly white neighborhood we live in.

If hearing Hagerman's long list is discouraging to you, I encourage you to start where you can, and then keep going. This is not work that we accomplish in a few weeks or months. It is work that's ongoing. Even when our children are grown, our own antiracist journeys will continue.

In a workshop on confronting our social class privilege, my friend Rev. Lucy Waechter Webb introduced me to an important idea. She drew the graphic you see below. She explained that our goal for the workshop was to move beyond our comfort zone into the circle of growth.

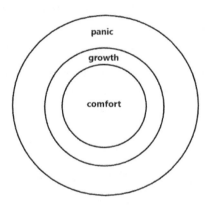

However, we can only attempt so much growth at one time before we will bump into the much thicker circle of panic. Because pushing ourselves to change too quickly leads to panic and burnout, we'll retreat all the way back to the comfort zone.

As we think about the changes we will make, we can focus on those that require us to stretch and grow but do not push us into panic. We can start where we are and continually press ourselves to take that work a little further than feels comfortable. Figuring out how to take action, without feeling like I must say yes to every request, is a continual balancing act.

There are times when I realize I've become too wrapped up in my own family life and neglected the larger community I'm part of. Other times, I've jumped into so many causes that I ended up burnout and inactive for months at a time.

When I'm not sure what I should be doing, I remind myself that the struggle to dismantle racism needs my participation long term. I also try not to get too caught up in my head. I ask myself whether white supremacist perfectionism is shaping my choices. **I've also seen many times how perfectionism shows up in white people as an obsession over process.**

If you find yourself struggling for months over where you should focus your activism, or you are wondering endlessly about how to have a particular conversation about race with your child, recognize that perfectionism is rearing its ugly head. As someone who's prone to this myself, I urge you: refuse to get stuck.

Don't worry about making the perfect antiracist choice. Focus on finding a good choice and put that choice into action. You can always go back and improve on what you started.

Practice: Choose an action within your sphere of influence

You may have a child who is even more eager than you to challenge racism. You may have a child who's not interested in activism at all. No matter where your child is in this moment, you can commit to taking your own action in at least one area of your life.

As parents we're juggling a lot, so I recommend finding just one place to start, and committing to taking action in that particular space regularly. When you think about the impact of racism, what hurts your heart the most? What do you most long to see transformed? Perhaps it's police brutality, or immigrant families being torn apart by deportations. Whatever pains you is sure to have disturbed others as well.

Your first action step could be signing up for the email list of a social justice group addressing that issue, and pledging that when they ask you to call, write, or show up, you will do that to the best of your ability.

If you're already taking action in this way and you long for something more in-depth, consider where you already spend your time. For some parents, that will be at their child's school or in the larger school district. Are there parents of color who have been voicing their concerns about academic tracking being racially biased? Perhaps other parents are concerned about how racial bias affects school discipline.

Does the PTA at your school mostly reflect the concerns of white middle class parents? If so, how can you amplify the voices of parents of color? What changes need to happen to make the group one that more parents of color want to participate in?

At a smaller level, you might talk with your child's teacher about what curriculum is being used and what books are available to children in the classroom.

You might prefer to start in your own workplace, encouraging your employer to make antiracist changes in your company's culture.

Perhaps your house of worship is the best place to take action. In my segregated city, I'm often struck by what traumatizing news events are prayed about in Sunday worship in Black and Latinx churches, while those same events aren't even mentioned in white churches. At a deeper level, what justice organizations would welcome a partnership with your congregation?

Spiritual and emotional foundations for antiracism

I understand racial justice to be a spiritual practice, a healing practice, a heart practice. The keyword being practice. To me, anti-racism at its root is a practice of reconnecting to self and to others. The primary strategy that guilt, shame and fear have in common is to generate disconnection and isolation. Therefore, I understand that our primary strategy has to be to generate connection through relationship and action. It is not possible to solely think our way out of white supremacy, we must also feel our way out. Staying in my heart and in connection with beloved community as much as possible helps me to practice doing this imperfectly everyday.

—Jes Kelley, in *Practice Showing Up: A Guidebook for White People Working for Racial Justice* by Jardana Peacock[63]

People vary widely in their relationship to religion, but I believe that all of us have an innate spirituality, whether we are part of a religious community or not. When we fail to root ourselves in that spirituality, it's far too easy to burn out and abandon the antiracist journey we've started.

Years ago, when I was an overwhelmed community organizer and on the verge of burnout, I invited others

from our organization to join a weekly prayer and Bible study group. In that space, we became even more of a community that we had been. Though we'd always been a faith-rooted organization, this was the place we could voice our fears and hopes in honest and authentic ways.

In 2019, I promised myself I would take a deeper look at how white supremacy shapes me by working through Layla Saad's *Me and White Supremacy Workbook.* The workbook required me to look inward in a way that was more challenging than any antiracism work I'd done to that point.

I know without a doubt, I would have abandoned the workbook if I hadn't made space for prayer and yoga, so that I could process the things I was realizing about myself. There were days when the moment I finished writing in the workbook, I had to unroll my yoga mat to work through the shame and sadness I was feeling.

This summer as I processed a change in our family's life that we were making because of our antiracist commitment, I was grieving. A retreat with other white antiracist activists reminded me that my favorite form of prayer, especially when I need hope, has always been singing. Since then, I've made time to sing hymns and social justice movement songs on a regular basis, so that I can show up as my whole self in the struggle against racism.

As your family continues the journey of antiracism, I encourage you to show up with your whole self. Root yourself in spiritual practices and share some of those practices with your children. Make time to connect with your body. Seek connection with other people, not just at an intellectual level, but at the heart level as well.

Do these things because you are needed in the antiracist struggle, not just in this moment, but for a lifetime.

Things to remember

- Knowing the stage of racial identity development helps us understand the many emotions and reactions that both we and our kids will have on our antiracist journeys.

- The desire to be perfect is rooted in white supremacy culture. We must remember that making a mistake is not the same as being a mistake.

- As antiracist parents, we are most effective when make changes that pull us out of our comfort zone into growth, but that do not push us into panic.

- Finding community support and spiritual resources are crucial to keeping us in the work of antiracism for the long haul.

Conclusion
Can we live for the we?

Not long ago, a white friend and I were talking about the challenges of trying to parent our kids in an antiracist way. In our segregated and conservative city, it's incredibly easy for to take advantage of all the choices that white privilege makes available to us. It takes intentional decision after decision to raise white kids in an antiracist manner.

Sometimes our choices will inspire other white parents to make their own hard decisions. Other times, our choices will baffle or even anger other white parents. For me, returning to the vision of who I want my sons to become makes it possible for me to make hard choices.

I am learning, slowly, to break the silence I've been taught to keep as a white person. With my child and on my own, I'm spending more time than ever learning American history as it actually happened, not the whitewashed version that I was taught in school.

I'm making more deliberate choices about what issues I advocate for. My husband and I are thinking about how to shift the places and groups of people we spend our time with so that our lives are less segregated.

As I make these choices, I have to go beyond the question of what is best for my children's future success. I also have to ask the question, "What choices make sense if I want kids of color to have the same security, respect, and opportunities to thrive that my white children enjoy?"

At times these choices feel painful, especially when

I'm not sure if other white parents understand them. But just as often, I feel hope and joy. I see the ways that my family doesn't have to follow the expected pattern for upper middle-class white Americans. My main goal as a parent doesn't have to be accumulating advantages for my nuclear family alone.

I see the brave ways that antiracist parents of all races are refusing to structure their lives according to the lies that racism tells us. They are breaking free of racism's hold on them, and they inspire me to do the same.

During seminary I kept a quote book where I jotted down the words of theologians, activists, and writers that sustained my vision for social justice. Twelve years before I became a mother, I was engrossed in the writings of Dorothee Soelle. She was a German theologian whose faith and whose experience of motherhood compelled her to become deeply involved in resisting the Vietnam War.

In my quote book, I recorded her perceptive words from her memoir *Against the Wind:* "I realized that 'motherliness' is indivisible; one cannot be a mother to one or two or three children and that's it."

I was reminded of this sentiment when I encountered Dani McClain's book, *We Live for the We: The Political Power of Black Motherhood.* McClain takes the title from a conversation she had with Cat Brooks, a Black mother and community organizer in Oakland.

When there are tough choices their family has to make between their own desires and the needs of their community, Brooks reminds her daughter that "we don't live for the I. We live for the we."[64] **If we are to dismantle racism, white parents must also learn to live for the "we."**

We must catch up to Black mothers and other

parents of color, who know that our family conversations and choices don't exist in a vacuum. Are we raising our children to recognize racism and injustice, and to resist them? Are we teaching them to show up, however imperfectly, for the world they want to see?

My hope and prayer each day, for you and for me, is that we will be able to answer those questions with a humble and hopeful, "Yes. I am doing the work, in all my imperfection. I am growing. I'm learning, more and more, to live for the we."[65]

Resources

Children's books about skin tone, race, and racism

For ages 0–3:

Manushkin, Fran and Lauren Tobia. *Happy In Our Skin.*

Pinkney, Andrea Davis and Brian Pinkney. *Pretty Brown Face.*

Tyler, Michael and David Lee Csicscko. *The Skin You Live In.*

For ages 3–6:

Genhart, Michael and Viviana Garofoli. *Ouch Moments: When Words Are Used in Hurtful Ways.*

Katz, Karen. *The Colors of Us.*

Kendi, Ibram X and Ashley Lukashevsky. *Antiracist Baby.*

Kissinger, Katie. *All the Colors We Are: The Story of How We Get Our Skin Tone.*

Mason, Margaret and Floyd Cooper. *These Hands.*

Miller, Sharee. *Don't Touch My Hair!*

Robertson, David. *When We Were Alone.*

Rotner, Shelley and Sheila M. Kelly. *Shades of People.*

Williamson, Dorena, Cornelius Van Wright, and Ying-Hwa Hu. *ColorFull: Celebrating the Colors God Gave Us.*

For ages 6–9:

Celano, Marianne, Marietta Collins, Ann Hazzard, and Jennifer Zivoin. *Something Happened in Our Town: A Child's Story about Racial Injustice.*

hooks, bell. *Skin Again.*

Lester, Julius and Karen Barbour. *Let's Talk about Race.*

Mobin-Uddin and Barbara Kiwak. *My Name is Bilal.*

Serres, Alain and Aurélia Fronty. *I Have the Right to Be a Child.*

For ages 9–12:

Colbert, Brandy. *The Only Black Girls in Town.*

Delacre, Lulu. *Us, In Progress: Short Stories about Young Latinos.*

Draper, Sharon. *Stella by Starlight.*

Higginbotham, Anastasia. *Not My Idea: A Book about Whiteness.*

Johnson, Varian. *The Parker Inheritance.*

LaMotte, David and Jenn Hales. *White Flour.*

Peacock, Thomas and Marlene Wisuri. *To Be Free: Understanding and Eliminating Racism.*

For ages 12+:

Jewell, Tiffany. *This Book Is Anti-Racist: 20 Lessons on How to Wake Up, Take Action, and Do the Work.*

Quigley, Dawn. *Apple in the Middle.*

Reynolds, Jason and Ibram X. Kendi. *Stamped: Racism, Antiracism, and You.*

Smith, Cynthia Leitich. *Hearts Unbroken.*

Stevenson, Bryan. *Just Mercy (Adapted for Young Adults): A True Story of the Fight for Justice.*

Thomas, Angie. *The Hate U Give.*

Yang, Gene Luen. *American Born Chinese.*

Children's books about immigrant experiences

For ages 3–6:

O'Brien, Anne Sibley. *I'm New Here.*

For ages 6–9:

Choi, Yangsook. *The Name Jar.*

Danticat, Edwidge and Leslie Staub. *Mama's Nightingale: A Story of Immigration and Separation.*

Kuntz, Doug, Amy Shrodes, and Sue Cornelison. *Lost and Found Cat: The True Story of Kukkush's Incredible Journey.*

Mak, Kam. *My Chinatown: One Year in Poems.*

Mills, Deborah, Alfredo Alva, and Claudia Navarro. *La Frontera: My Journey with Papa.*

Morales, Yuyi. *Dreamers.*

Phi, Bao and Thi Bui. *A Different Pond.*

Quintero, Isabel and Zeke Peña. *My Papi Has a Motorcycle.*

Tonatiuh, Duncan. *Pancho Rabbit and the Coyote.*

Velasquez, Eric. *Grandma's Records.*

For ages 9–12:

Behar, Ruth. *Lucky Broken Girl.*

Kullab, Samya, Jackie Roche, and Mike Freiheit. *Escape from Syria.*

Respicio, Mae. *The House That Lou Built.*

Yang, Kelly. *Front Desk.*

Children's books about activism

For ages 3–6:

Browne, Mahogany L. and Theodore Taylor III. *Woke Baby.*

Evans, Shane W. *We March.*

McDaniel, Breanna and Shane W. Evans. *Hands Up!*

Nagara, Innosanto. *A is for Activist.*

For ages 6–9:

Asim, Jabari and E.B. Lewis. *Preaching to the Chickens: The Story of Young John Lewis.*

Braswell, Kenneth, Joe Dent, and Julie Anderson. *Daddy, There's a Noise Outside.*

Brown, Monica and Joe Cepeda. *Side by Side: The Story of Dolores Huerta and Cesar Chavez.*

Clark-Robinson, Monica and Frank Morrison. *Let the Children March.*

Kurusa and Monika Doppert. *The Streets Are Free.*

Pinkney, Andrea Davis and Brian Pinkney. *Boycott Blues: How Rosa Parks Inspired a Nation.*

Rhuday-Perkovich, Olugbemisola and Jade Johnson. *Someday Is Now: Clara Luper and the 1958 Oklahoma City Sit-Ins.*

Romito, Dee. *Pies from Nowhere: How Georgia Gilmore Sustained the Montgomery Bus Boycott.*

Tudor, Aslan and Kelly Tudor. *Young Water Protectors: A Story about Standing Rock.*

For ages 9–12:

Atkins, Laura, Stan Yogi, and Yutaka Houlette. *Fred Korematsu Speaks Up.*

Dias, Marley. *Marley Dias Gets It Done and So Can You!*

Duncan, Alice Faye and R. Gregory Christie. *Memphis, Martin, and the Mountaintop: The Sanitation Strike of 1968.*

Hendrix, John. *John Brown: His Fight for Freedom.*

Mulholland, Loki, Angela Fairwell, and Charlotta Janssen. *She Stood for Freedom: The Untold Story of a Civil Rights Hero, Joan Trumpauer Mulholland.*

Myers, Walter Dean and Bonnie Christensen. *Ida B. Wells: Let the Truth Be Told.*

Nagara, Innosanto. *The Wedding Portrait.*

Shabazz, Ilyasah and A.G. Ford. *Malcolm Little: The Boy Who Grew Up To Become Malcolm X.*

Weatherford, Carole Boston and Ekua Holmes. *Voice of Freedom: Fannie Lou Hamer, Spirit of the Civil Rights Movement.*

Williams-Garcia, Rita. *One Crazy Summer.*

For ages 13+:

Hoose, Phillip. *Claudette Colvin: Twice Toward Justice.*

Lewis, John. *March* trilogy.

Paul, Caroline and Lauren Tamaki. *You Are Mighty: A Guide to Changing the World.*

Wilson, Jamia and Andrea Pippins. *Step Into Your Power: 23 Lessons on How to Live Your Best Life.*

History books for kids written from the perspectives of people of color

For ages 0–3:

Harrison, Vashti. *Dream Big, Little One.*

For ages 3–6:

Barnes, Wiley and Aaron Long. *C Is for Chickasaw.*

Denise, Anika Aldamuy and Paola Escobar. *Planting Stories: The Life of Librarian and Storyteller Pura Belpré.*

Ringgold, Faith. *Aunt Harriet's Railroad in the Sky.*

Woodson, Jacqueline. *This is the Rope: A Story from the*

Great Migration.

For ages 6–9:

Alko, Selina and Sean Qualls. *The Case for Loving: The Fight for Interracial Marriage.*

Coulson, Art and Nick Hardcastle. *Unstoppable: How Jim Thorpe and the Carlisle Indian School Football Team Defeated Army.*

Hopkinson, Deborah and Don Tate. *Carter Reads the Newspaper.*

Hopkinson, Deborah and Ron Husband. *Steamboat School.*

Jordan-Fenton, Christy, Margaret Pokiak-Fenton, and Gabrielle Grimard. *Not My Girl.*

McPhaull, Delina Pryce. *Oh Freedom! A Conscious U.S. History Curriculum.* (Find at wokehomeschooling.com)

Mochizuki, Ken and Dom Lee. *Baseball Saved Us.*

Moss, Marissa and Carl Angel. *Sky High: The Story of Maggie Gee.*

Ramsey, Calvin Alexander, Gwen Strauss, and Floyd Cooper. *Ruth and the Green Book.*

Ringgold, Faith. *We Came to America.*

Tingle, Tim and Jeanne Rorex Bridges. *Crossing Bok Chitto: A Choctaw Tale of Friendship and Freedom.*

Tonatiuh, Duncan. *Separate Is Never Equal: Sylvia Mendez and Her Family's Fight for Desegregation.*

Tate, Don. *Poet: The Remarkable Story of George Moses Horton.*

Weatherford, Carole Boston and R. Gregory Christie.

Freedom in Congo Square.

Weatherford, Carole Boston and Jamey Christoph. *Gordon Parks: How the Photographer Captured Black and White America.*

Winter, Jonah and Shane Evans. *Lillian's Right to Vote: A Celebration of the Voting Rights Act of 1965.*

Yoo, Paula and Dom Lee. *Sixteen Years in Sixteen Seconds: The Sammy Lee Story.*

For ages 9–12:

Chambers, Veronica. *Finish the Fight: The Brave and Revolutionary Women Who Fought for the Right to Vote.*

Conkling, Winifred. *Sylvia and Aki.*

Crowe, Ellie and Richard Waldrep. *Surfer of the Century: The Life of Duke Kahanamoku.*

Dupuis, Jenny Kay, Kathy Kacer, and Gillian Newland. *I Am Not a Number.*

Erdrich, Louie. *The Birchbark House.* (series)

Lyle, Tom. *Chickasaw Adventures: The Complete Collection.*

Mcmanis, Charlene Willing and Traci Sorell. *Indian No More.*

Munoz Ryan, Pam. *Esperanza Rising.*

Nelson, Kadir. *Heart and Soul: The Story of America and African Americans.*

Ortiz, Simon and Sharol Graves. *The People Shall Continue.*

Perry, Anthony. *Chula the Fox.*

Robertson, Robbie and David Shannon. *Hiawatha and the*

Peacemaker.

Robertson, Sebastian and Adam Gustavson. *Rock and Roll Highway: The Robbie Robertson Story.*

Weatherford, Carole Boston and Eric Velasquez. *Schomburg: The Man Who Built a Library.*

For ages 13+:

Dionne, Evette. *Lifting As We Climb: Black Women's Battle for the Ballot Box.*

Dunbar, Erica Armstrong and Kathleen Van Cleve. *Never Caught: The Story of Ona Judge (Young Readers Edition.)*

Dunbar-Ortiz, Rozanne and Debbie Reese. *An Indigenous People's History of the United States for Young People.*

Everyday stories: children's books starring kids of color

Arab and Asian

For ages 0–3:

Park, Linda Sue and Ho Baek Lee. *Bee-Bim Bop!*

Singh, Rina. *Holi Colors.*

Suen, Anastasia and Winnie Cheon. *Toddler Two.*

For ages 3–6:

Khan, Hena and Mehrdokht Amini. *Golden Domes and Silver Lanterns: A Muslim Book of Colors.*

Khan, Rukhsana and Sophie Blackall. *Big Red Lollipop.*

Le, Minh and Dan Santat. *Drawn Together.*

For ages 6–9:

English, Karen and Jonathan Weiner. *Nadia's Hands.*

Low, A.J. *Sherlock Sam and the Missing Heirloom in Katong.* (series)

Martin, Jacqueline Briggs and June Jo Lee. *Chef Roy Choi and the Street Food Remix.*

Michiko Florence, Debbi and Elizabet Vukovic. *Jasmine Toguchi, Mochi Queen.* (series)

Nye, Naomi Shihab and Nancy Carpenter. *Sitti's Secrets.*

Pak, Soyung and Susan Kathleen Hartung. *Dear Juno.*

For ages 9–12:

Khan, Hena. *Amina's Voice.*

Lai, Remy. *Pie in the Sky.*

Shang, Wendy Wan-Long. *The Great Wall of Lucy Wu.*

Yang, Kelly. *Front Desk.* (series)

Black

Ages 0–3:

Asim, Jabari and LeUyen Pham. *Whose Toes Are Those?*

Lee, Spike, Tonya Lewis Lee, and Kadir Nelson. *Please, Baby, Please.*

McQuinn, Anna and Ruth Hearson. *Leo Loves Baby Time.*

Ages 3–6:

Barnes, Derrick and Vanessa Brantley Newton. *The King of Kindergarten.*

Frederickson, Lane and Michael Robertson. *Monster Trouble.*

Morrison, Toni, Slade Morrison, and Joe Cepeda. *Peeny Butter Fudge.*

Schofield-Morrison, Connie and Frank Morrison. *I Got the Rhythm.*

Ages 6–9:

Cameron, Ann. *The Stories Julian Tells.* (series)

Dumas, Marti and Marie Muravski. *Jaden Toussaint, The Greatest.* (series)

English, Karen. *Nikki and Deja* (series).

Harrington, Janice and Shelley Jackson. *The Chicken Chasing Queen of Lamar County.*

For ages 9–12:

Craft, Jerry. *The New Kid.* (series)

Draper, Sharon. *The Clubhouse Mysteries.* (series)

Elliott, Zetta. *Dragons in a Bag.* (series)

Magoon, Kekla. *The Seasons of Styx Malone.*

Woodsen, Jacqueline. *Brown Girl Dreaming.*

Latinx

For ages 0–3:

Tafolla, Carmen and Magaly Morales. *What Can You Do With a Paleta?*

Thong, Roseanna Greenfield and John Parra. *Green Is a Chile Pepper: A Book of Colors.*

For ages 3–6:

Manning, Maurie. *Kitchen Dance.*

Martinez-Neal, Juana. *Alma and How She Got Her Name.*

Mora, Pat and Cecily Lang. *Pablo's Tree.*

Morales, Yuyi. *Rudas: Niño's Horrendous Hermanitas.*

Ryan, Pam Muñoz and Joe Cepeda. *Mice and Beans.*

Velasquez, Eric. *Looking for Bongo.*

For ages 6–9:

Ada, Alma Flor and Elivia Savadier. *I Love Saturdays y domingos.*

Brown, Monica and Angela Dominguez. *Lola Levine Is Not Mean!* (series)

Quintero, Isabel and Zeke Peña. *My Papi Has a Motorcycle.*

Velasquez, Eric. *Grandma's Gift.*

For ages 9–12:

Alvarez, Julia. *How Tía Lola Came to Stay.* (series)

Cartaya, Pablo. *The Epic Fail of Arturo Zamora.*

Elliott, Zetta. *Max Loves Muñecas.*

Pérez, Celia. *The First Rule of Punk.*

For ages 13+:

Acevedo, Elizabeth. *The Poet X.*

Native American/Indigenous

For ages 0–3:

Tahe, RoseAnn, Nancy Bo Flood, and Jonathan Nelson. *First Laugh, Welcome Baby!*

Van Camp, Richard and Julie Flatt. *We Sang You Home.*

For ages 3–6:

Child, Brenda J., Jonathan Thunder, and Gordon Jourdain. *Bowwow Powwow.*

Kalluk, Celina and Alexandria Neonakis. *Sweetest Kulu.*

Sorrell, Traci and Frané Lessac, *We Are Grateful: Otsaliheliga.*

For ages 6–9:

Smith, Cynthia Leitich. *Indian Shoes.*

Smith, Cynthia Leitich, Cornelius Van Wright, and Ying-Hwa Hu. *Jingle Dancer.*

Uluadluak, Donald and Qin Leng. *Kamik: An Inuit Puppy Story.*

For ages 9–12:

Smith, Cynthia Leitich. *Rain Is Not My Indian Name.*

Vandever, Daniel W. *Fall In Line, Holden!*

Multicultural

For ages 0–3:

Blackstone, Stella. *Baby Talk.*

Global Fund for Children. *Global Babies.*

Williams, Vera B. *More More More Said the Baby.*

For ages 3–6:

Smith, Anita Hope. *My Daddy Rules the World: Poems about Dads.*

Strickland, Tessa, Kate DePalma, and David Dean. *Barefoot Books Children of the World.*

For ages 6–9:

Woodson, Jacqueline. *The Day You Begin.*

For ages 9–12:

Tarpley, Natasha. *The Harlem Charade.*

Woodson, Jacqueline. *Harbor Me.*

Multicultural children's toys and media

Toy makers

- Elle and Cee World Girls ecworldgirls.com (Black owned)

- Ikuzi Dolls. ikuzidolls.com (Black owned)

- Jambo Books monthly subscription boxes. jambobooks.com (Black owned)

- My Family Builders. myfamilybuilders.com

- Toys Like Me. toyslikeme.com (Black owned)

Find additional multicultural toy and gift ideas at rebekahgienapp.com/multicultural-toys/

Children's shows

- *Bino and Fino.* (Some episodes available for streaming on Amazon Prime.)

- *Bookmarks: Celebrating Black Voices.* (Netflix)

- *Doc McStuffins.* (Disney Junior)

- *Molly of Denali.* (PBS)

- *Motown Magic.* (Netflix)

- *Nella the Princess Knight.* (Nickleodeon)

- *Nina's World.* (can be streamed on several platforms)

- *Pocoyo.* (Netflix, PBS)

- *Raising Dion.* (Netflix)

Children's Music

- *The Love,* by the Alphabet Rockers.
  alphabetrockers.com
- A playlist of social justice songs for children.
  rebekahgienapp.com/socia-justice-songs

Resources on race and racism for adults

Books about children, parenting, and race

Brandt, Cindy Wang. *Parenting Forward: How to Raise Children with Justice, Mercy, and Kindness.*

Derman-Sparks, Louise and Julie Olsen Edwards. *Anti-Bias Education for Young Children and Ourselves.*

Hagerman, Margaret. *White Kids: Growing Up with Privilege in a Racially Divided America.*

Harvey, Jennifer. *Raising White Kids: Bringing Up Children in a Racially Unjust America.*

McClain, Dani. *We Live for the We: The Political Power of Black Motherhood.*

Tatum, Beverly Daniel. *Why Are All the Black Kids Sitting Together in the Cafeteria? and Other Conversations about Race.*

Articles about children, parenting, and race

"Beyond the Golden Rule: A Parent's Guide to Preventing and Responding to Prejudice," from Teaching Tolerance. tolerance.org/sites/default/files/general/beyond_golden_rul e.pdf

"Decolonizing Thanksgiving: A Toolkit for Combatting

Racism in Schools," by Lindsey Passenger Wieck. medium.com/age-of-awareness/decolonizing-thanksgiving-a-toolkit-for-combatting-racism-in-schools-5d4e3023a2f8

"Why We Don't Wear Mohawks," by Lisa Graustein. medium.com/@LisaGraustein/why-we-dont-wear-mohawks-a-conversation-about-who-we-are-and-cultural-appropriation-with-my-7-ddcd6dcfc666

"Moana, Elsa, and Halloween," by Sachi Feris. raceconscious.org/2017/09/moana-elsa-halloween/

"Talking about Cultural Appropriation with Young Children," by Katie Norris. https://thebodyisnotanapology.tumblr.com/post/993144597 61/talking-about-cultural-appropriation-with-young

Teaching for Change's Resources on Ensuring Equity in Parent Organizations. https://www.teachingforchange.org/parent-organizing/equityinparentorgs

"Don't Integrate Schools Just to Benefit White Kids" by ShaRonda Knotts Dawson. https://educationpost.org/dont-integrate-schools-just-to-benefit-white-kids/

General books about racism

DiAngelo, Robin. *White Fragility: Why It's So Hard for White People to Talk about Racism.*

Dunbar-Ortiz, Roxanne. *An Indigenous Peoples' History of the United States.*

Kendi, Ibram X. *How to Be an Antiracist.*

Kivel, Paul. *Uprooting Racism: How White People Can Work for Racial Justice.*

Oluo, Ijeoma. *So You Want to Talk about Race.*

Saad, Layla. *Me and White Supremacy: Combat Racism, Change the World, and Become a Good Ancestor.*

Treuer, Anton. *Everything You Wanted to Know about Indians but Were Afraid to Ask.*

Wilkerson, Isabel. *Caste: The Origins of Our Discontents.*

Books on spirituality and antiracism

DeLeon-Hartshotrn, Iris, Tobin Miller Shearer, and Regina Shands Stotfus. *Set Free: A Journey Toward Solidarity Against Racism.*

Harvey, Jennifer. *Dear White Christians: For Those Still Longing for Racial Reconciliation*

Peacock, Jardana. *Practice Showing Up: A Guidebook for White People Working for Racial Justice.*

Finding community with other antiracist parents

Raising Antiracist Kids Caregiver Reflection Circle

Twice a year I offer a 5 week interactive reflection series that not only helps parents and teachers build their skills in raising white kids to be antiracist, but also creates connection between participants. Because there are a maximum of 16 participants at a time, those who in enroll have many opportunities to dialogue and offer support to each other, both during the series and beyond. Learn more at rebekahgienapp.com/reflect

Embrace Race

Embrace Race is a nonprofit organization and a multiracial community of parents, teachers, experts, and other caring adults who support each other to meet the challenges that race poses to our children, families, and communities. They offer monthly online workshops on a variety of topics related to kids and race. Please consider donating to their work as a way to support healthy racial development for children of color. embracerace.org

Integrated Schools

Integrated Schools is a movement of white and privileged parents who are choosing to enroll their children in public schools in which they are not the majority. They offer many resources on their website, as well as a Facebook group for parents who have enrolled their children in an integrating school. If you are considering enrolling your child in an integrating school, you can request to speak to another parent about their experience. There are also a number of chapters across the United States. Integratedschools.org

Showing Up for Racial Justice.

SURJ is a national network of groups and individuals working to undermine white supremacy and to work toward racial justice. Through community organizing, mobilizing, and education, SURJ moves white people to act as part of a multi-racial majority for justice with passion and accountability, with chapters across the United States. You can also find resources particular to families at showingupforracialjustice.org/surj-families.html

Acknowledgements

The process of writing this book has been daunting. This is my first book, and the first time doing something is always challenging. But mostly it was daunting because I was writing about a topic that makes many people uneasy. It was challenging because I was offering readers a much deeper look into my life and my parenting than I provide on my blog.

There are so many people who have supported me in this project and who have made this book much better than it would have otherwise been. I'm so grateful to the readers who provided feedback on early drafts: Helen Anderson, Maryam T. Brotine, Megan Fischer, Lois Johnson-Mead, Courtney M., Stephanie Phippen, Claire Prince, Cindy Hastings Sakaan, and Natacha W.

I'm humbled and honored by the mentors and colleagues who provided feedback and offered their endorsement of this project: Lucretia Berry, Marietta Collins, Andrew Grant-Thomas, Jennifer Harvey, Ann Hazzard, and Jardana Peacock.

For the children, families, and staff of St. John's United Methodist Church, Evergreen Presbyterian Church, and the Peace Camp community, thank you for your grace in allowing me to learn and teach at the same time. Special thanks to Mitchel Griffin, Linda Hamilton, and Lucy Waechter-Webb.

For my blog readers and community, who asked questions again and again about navigating kids and race. You prompted me to write about this topic before I felt truly ready, and for that I am grateful.

For all the friends and family who told me early on

that what I had to share was indeed helpful, who offered critiques and pushback when I needed it, who shared their parenting and race struggles, and who checked in often to ask "how's the writing going?" Thank you Alexa, Anne, Annie, Claire, Courtney, Faiqa, Hunter, Janel, Melissa, Michael, Mimi, Rorie, Sally, and Shauna (and lots of other people I'm forgetting to name!)

For my parents, Craig and Kay Jordan, who gave me brave examples in my childhood of how to wrestle with race, who have been willing to unlearn racism beside me in adulthood, and whose faith in me has been unfailing.

To my boys: thank you for letting me try and make mistakes and learn and see the world through your eyes. Thank you for listening, for asking questions, and being brave. I'm so lucky to be your mom.

For my husband Andy: there aren't words enough. For being my rock, for allowing me space to pursue this dream, for helping me keep going despite my doubts, for the hours you spent editing and tinkering in Photoshop, for being a partner in every sense of the word: thank you and I love you.

About the author

Rebekah Gienapp is a writer, speaker, and parenting coach. Her work focuses on nurturing a commitment to social justice and antiracism in children, especially those whose families hold privilege. Her work has been featured by *The Washington Post*, Parenting Forward, and *MLK50: Justice Through Journalism*. She is ordained in the United Methodist Church, and lives with her family in Memphis, Tennessee.

More of her writing can be found at rebekahgienapp.com

Contacting Rebekah

If you'd like to receive regular updates and free resources designed for parents and educators who care about social justice and antiracism from Rebekah, sign up for her email list.

When you download the free pack of bonus worksheets created to go with this book, you'll also be added to the email list. Download the bonus pack at antiracistkids.com.

You can share your questions and feedback with Rebekah, as well as inquire about scheduling her to present an antiracist kids workshop to your organization by emailing rebekah@thebarefootmommy.com.

[1] Erin Winkler, "Why Does Latin@ Youth Literature Matter? How Children Learn About Race," in *Honoring Latin@ Children's and Young Adult Literature of the Americas,* ed. Laretta Henderson (Lanham: Lexington Books, 2016), 8–9.
[2] American Psychological Assocation, RESilience: Uplifting Youth Through Health Communication about Race, https://www.apa.org/res/parent-resources/reading (accessed September 25, 2019).

[3] Louise Derman-Sparks and Julie Olsen Edwards, *Anti-Bias Education for Young Children and Ourselves.* (Washington: National Association for the Education of Young Children, 2010), 14–15.

[4] Po Bronson and Ashley Merryman, *NurtureShock: New Thinking About Children* (New York: Twelve, 2009), 47–51.

[5] Erin Winkler, "Why Does Latin@ Youth Literature Matter? How Children Learn About Race," 19.

[6] Jennifer Harvey, *Raising White Kids: Bringing Up Children in a Racially Unjust America* (Nashville: Abingdon Press, 2017), 50–51.

[7] Ibram X. Kendi, *How To Be an Antiracist* (New York: One World, 2019), 9.

[8] Ibid., 13.

[9] Bronson and Merryman, *NurtureShock,* 54.

[10] Kim Sherman, "On the Spot: Unanticipated Conversations About Race," *Raising Race Conscious Children,* http://www.raceconscious.org/2015/11/on-the-spot-unanticipated-conversations-about-race/

[11] Rebekah Gienapp, "How Should We Respond to Racism in Dr. Seuss Books?" *The Barefoot Mommy,* https://www.thebarefootmommy.com/2019/03/racism-dr-seuss/

[12] "The Powerful Lesson Maya Angelou Taught Oprah," http://www.oprah.com/oprahs-lifeclass/the-powerful-lesson-maya-angelou-taught-oprah-video
[13] Sachi Feris, "Explaining 'Race' vs. Skin Color to My Three Year Old," *Raising Race Conscious Children,* http://www.raceconscious.org/2015/12/explaining-race-versus-skin-color-to-my-three-year-old/
[14] Harvey, *Raising White Kids,* 79.

[15] Derman-Sparks and Edwards, *Anti-Bias Education for Young Children and Ourselves*, 81.

[16] *Raising Race Conscious Children,* http://www.raceconscious.org/2017/03/interrupting-whiteness-white-family/ (accessed September 25, 2019.)

[17] Harvey, *Raising White Kids,* 8.

[18] *Black Lives Matter at School,* http://weac.org/wp-content/uploads/2018/02/kid-friendly-language.pdf (accessed September 25, 2019).

[19] Di'Angelo, Robin. "White Fragility," *Journal of Critical Pedagogy*, Volume 3 (3) (2011), 54.

[20] Derman-Sparks and Edwards, *Anti-Bias Education for Young Children and Ourselves*, 87.

[21] Erin Winkler, "Why Does Latin@ Youth Literature Matter? How Children Learn About Race," 10.

[22] Bronson and Merryman, *NurtureShock,* 55.

[23] Kendi, *How To Be an Antiracist*, 53.

[24] Ijeoma Oluo, *So You Want to Talk About Race*, (Seal Press, 2018), 11.

[25] Harvey, *Raising White Kids*, 261.

[26] Michael Safi. "Statue of 'racist' Gandhi removed from University of Ghana," *The Guardian*, December 14, 2018, https://www.theguardian.com/world/2018/dec/14/racist-gandhi-statue-removed-from-university-of-ghana

[27] Sydella Blatch, "Great achievements in science and technology in ancient Africa," *American Society for Biochemistry and Moceular Biology*, https://www.asbmb.org/asbmbtoday/asbmbtoday_article.aspx?id=32437 (accessed September 25, 2019).

[28] Harvey, *Raising White Kids,* 142.

[29] Kristen Weir, "Inequality at School: What's Behind the Racial Disparity in Our Education System?" *Monitor on Pscyhology ,* November 2016, https://www.apa.org/monitor/2016/11/cover-inequality-school

[30] Kendi, *How To Be an Antiracist*, 22.

[31] Southern Poverty Law Center, *Speak Up: Responding to Everyday Bigotry*, https://www.splcenter.org/sites/default/files/d6_legacy_files/downloads/publication/splcspeak_up_handbook_0.pdfhttps://www.splcenter.org/20150125/speak-responding-everyday-bigotry (accessed September 25, 2019).

[32] Beverly Daniel Tatum, *Why Are All the Black Kids Sitting Together in the Cafeteria? And Other Conversations About Race,* (New York: Basic Books, 2017), 91.

[33] Harvey, *Raising White Kids*, 237.

[34] Margaret A. Hagerman, *White Kids: Growing Up With Privilege in a Racially Divided America*, (New York: New York University Press, 2018), 71.

[35] Tatum, *Why Are All the Black Kids Sitting Together in the Cafeteria?*, 133.

[36] Hagerman, *White Kids*, 9–10.

[37] Ibid., 31.

[38] Ibid., 106–107.

[39] Ibid., 108.
[40] Carrie Hutchinson, "Kids' Misuse of the Term 'Racist' Is Dangerous – So Let's Disrupt It," *The Establishment,* February 15, 2018, https://theestablishment.co/kids-misuse-of-the-term-racist-is-dangerous-so-let-s-disrupt-it-95235fb9a5fe/
[41] Harvey, *Raising White Kids*, 224.
[42] Kendi, *How To Be an Antiracist*,20.
[43] Ibid., 23.
[44] Education Post, *"2015 Parent Attitudes Survey,"* https://343jii21wly33h03em3o8es6-wpengine.netdna-ssl.com/wp-content/uploads/2015/10/Ed-Post-2015-Parent-Attitudes-Survey.pdf
[45] Sarah-SoonLing Blackburn, "What Is the Model Minority Myth?" *Teaching Tolerance,* March 21, 2019, https://www.tolerance.org/magazine/what-is-the-model-minority-myth
[46] https://zerflin.com/item/slavery-long-ago/
[47] Hagerman, *White Kids*, 105.
[48] Hagerman, *White Kids*, 117.
[49] Harvey, *Raising White Kids,* 232.

[50] Loretta J. Ross, "Speaking Up Without Tearing Down," *Teaching Tolerance,* Spring 2019, https://www.tolerance.org/magazine/spring-2019/speaking-up-without-tearing-down

[51] https://youtu.be/T_RTnuJvg6U

[52] Tatum, *Why Are All the Black Kids Sitting Together in the Cafeteria?*, 188.

[53] Tatum, *Why Are All the Black Kids Sitting Together in the Cafeteria?*, 189–193.

[54] Tatum, *Why Are All the Black Kids Sitting Together in the Cafeteria?*, 194–196.

[55] Tatum, *Why Are All the Black Kids Sitting Together in the Cafeteria?*, 199.

[56] Tatum, *Why Are All the Black Kids Sitting Together in the Cafeteria?*, 206.

[57] Harvey, *Raising White Kids,* 117.

[58] Tatum, *Why Are All the Black Kids Sitting Together in the Cafeteria?*, 201.

[59] Harvey, *Raising White Kids,* 120.

[60] Kenneth Jones and Tema Okun, "The Characteristics of White Supremacy Culture," *Dismantling Racism: A Workbook for Social Change Groups* (ChangeWorkd, 2001) posted at https://www.showingupforracialjustice.org/white-supremacy-culture-characteristics.html (accessed September 25, 2019).

[61] Ibid.

[62] Hagerman, *White Kids*, 206.

[63] Jardana Peacock, *Practice Showing Up: A Guidebook for White People Working for Racial Justice,* (2016), 22.

[64] Dani McClain, *We Live For the We: The Political Power of Black Motherhood,* (New York: Bold Type Books, 2019), 4.

Made in the USA
Monee, IL
31 January 2021